# Search for the New Land

The Dial Press | New York | 1969

# Julius Lester

# Search for the New Land

## History as Subjective Experience

(The title is taken from a composition
by jazz musician Lee Morgan, who has
recorded it on an album of the same name.)


Small portions of this book
appeared, in different form, in
*Sing Out* and *Katallegate*.

*For*
NEG
who came in the mail
*and*
Ron and Cheryll,
the H.N.I.C.

## NOTE

The poems in this book, except for one, are taken verbatim from newspapers and magazines where they appeared as news articles. I have simply arranged these articles, or portions of them, in poetic form. Such a technique has been called "found poetry," or "pop poetry." Neither appellation impresses me as being adequate to describe such poems, but I have no substitute to offer. Although academicians, critics, poets and others will be insulted, I call them poems, aware that I am stretching the meaning of a word which is already stretched out of shape.

By using news articles in such a way, the meaning of these articles has not been distorted. Quite the contrary. If anything, the meaning has been heightened. We are so accustomed to reading horror in each day's newspapers, the news columns bordered by ads, that we have become insensitive to that horror. By taking news articles and arranging them as poems, what was merely news in one context becomes the human experience it really is.

The one poem in the book which is an exception to the above is the poem beginning "The/mud/of/Vietnam," which is an original poem written during my trip to North Vietnam in 1967.

J. L.

You, who shall emerge from the flood
In which we are sinking,
Think—
When you speak of our weaknesses,
Also of the dark time
That brought them forth . . .

Even the hatred of squalor
Makes the brow grow stern.
Even anger against injustice
Makes the voice grow harsh. Alas, we
Who wished to lay the foundations of kindness
Could not ourselves be kind.

But you, when at last it comes to pass
That man can help his fellow man,
Do not judge us
Too harshly.

*Bertolt Brecht*

# one

# 1.

The sixties is what happens when a child looks at his parents and hates what he sees.

## PARENTS

Linda failed to return home from a dance Friday night.
On Saturday
she admitted she had spent the night
with an Air Force lieutenant.

The Aults decided on a punishment
that would "wake Linda up."
They ordered her
to shoot the dog
she had owned about two years.

On Sunday,
the Aults and
Linda
took the dog into the desert
near their home.
They
had the girl
dig a shallow grave.
Then
Mrs. Ault
grasped the dog between her hands and
Mr. Ault
gave
his daughter
a .22 caliber pistol
and told her
to shoot the dog.

Instead,
the girl
put the pistol
to her right temple
and shot herself.

The police said
there were no charges
that could be filed
against the parents
except possibly

cruelty
to
animals.

(*The New York Times*—February 7, 1968)

The youth of the sixties refused to learn the lessons of compromise and rationalization which define maturity in this society. They had no choice because they were unlike any generation in the history of the world; they had come to consciousness knowing that the world could be destroyed.

They knew little of idyllic childhood days when girls transformed themselves into queens in the blinking of an eye and the world was a crystal palace flashing with diadems of light. Their lives were like so many stalks of wheat waiting for the silent swish of the scythe. (Janie was sixteen when I met her at Camp Woodland in 1961 and one day, one rainy day when scudding clouds shrouded the peaks of the Catskill Mountains, she came to me. "Do you think there's going to be a world forever?" Being black the question hadn't occurred to me. If white folks wanted to blow up the world, they weren't about to ask my opinion. I told her I didn't know. "I want to have children when I grow up and I'm afraid they'll blow up the world before I do." And then she cried.) They knew nothing of the days when a life was no bigger than the city in which one lived. (The summer of 1962 dribbled into autumn and I had just been fired from a secretarial job at *Eros* magazine. It mattered little, for into the drabness of my West End Avenue furnished room had come a woman, a woman whom I loved, a woman whom I would marry in a few short months. No more would there be the days of trying to imagine how that one's hair would feel between my fingers or how that one's breasts would sing in the whorls of my fingertips. There was a woman in my life whom I loved. That was what was so different. A woman whom I loved. Not one I made myself love to fill the emptiness. We had only known each other a few months, a few delicious months of she and I in one room which was our world, a world where the sun never set and seagulls always soared.

October 24, 1962
1:45 A.M.

There may be a war. I hope I can write in here everyday until we know whether there will be war or not. I'd like to write something describing my reactions and feelings.

Yet, why should I write? If there is a war, there'll be no future generations to read what I write here. But, one must do something.

Last night, Monday, President Kennedy announced his quarantine on Cuba. My reaction and Joan's was one of horror. Today has been a day of fear for us. Russian ships are moving toward Cuba. U.S. ships have instructions to stop and search all ships going to Cuba. Those that refuse will be fired upon. Russia says they will not allow a search. Thus, the crisis.

All day we've read newspapers and listened to the radio, expecting to hear a declaration of war. She doesn't believe it will come. I do.

It may sound silly, but she and I have pledged that in case of war, we will stick together, no matter what. It may *sound* silly, but it doesn't feel silly or romantic or adolescent. It's not silly when you go to bed at night, knowing that you have no control over what happens tomorrow. What can you do? Love each other and write in your journal.

And yet, people went to work today. She and I went to the movies tonight. She went to classes. What else can one do?

We were reduced to two pathetic creatures in Kennedy's "finest hour.")

Gone forever were the days when a man looked at the ocean, a mountain or the sunset and felt his finiteness. Now he had only to read the paper to feel finite and insignificant, frighteningly alone. No longer did he have the illusion of being able to control or even understand his infinitesimal piece of existence. He could only sit and let it act upon him and when the confusion, the pain and the rage became too much, he would try to assert himself, to put things in order, the old order.

## THE WHITE MAN—I

Mrs. Pat Bates packed a
wicker basket with
chicken and
wine and
potato salad
today
and took her
9-year-old
daughter Patricia to her first
polo match.

"I wanted her to see it
while there was still time,"
said Mrs. Bates.
"We used to come here every
Sunday
when we were teen-agers.
And now
it's ending.

"Honestly,
everything
is
going
to
pot."

(*The New York Times*—October 16, 1967)

The youth who came to womanhood and manhood in the sixties knew the old order not as a cocoon of security, but as a weapon which left them (and all of us) whimpering with pain. When it came their turn to twist the dials and press the buttons, when it came their turn to undergo the apprenticeships before taking full command, they refused.

Any country is secure as long as its youth follow the way of the parents. If the young resist, the existence of that country is threatened. The youth of the sixties resisted.

### CALL TO ARMS

There is a time
when the operations of the machine
become so odious,
make you so sick at heart,
that you can't take part,
you can't even tacitly
take part.
And you've got to put your bodies
upon the gears
and upon the wheels,
upon the levers,
upon all the apparatus,
and you've got to make it
stop.

And you've got to indicate
to the people who run it,
to the people who own it,
that unless you're free
the machine
will be prevented
from working at all.

(Mario Savio at a rally on the
Berkeley campus of the University
of California, December, 1964.)

The time had come for the machine to be brought,
if not to a halt, at least to a long pause. It was past
time for someone in the country to live as if his
every breath depended on his adherence to basic
moral laws. If the scientists of the forties had done
so, there would have been no Hiroshima. If the
generation of the fifties had done so, there would
have been no McCarthy. But there was a Hiroshima;
there was a McCarthy. It was left to the generation
of the sixties to say what their parents had been
bribed out of saying, to do what their parents had
sold their lives not to do, to try and be what their
parents could have been.

It was their lives which were at stake and they
could no longer leave the responsibility for those
lives in adult hands. Didn't the scientists and techni-
cians at Los Alamos even think about their *own*
children as they worked everyday? Weren't the
physicists, in whose minds the atomic bomb became
real, able to go one tiny step further, see the consequences and say NO! Couldn't they extend themselves enough to say, "And what if this were done
to me?" If they had known and refused to say NO,

then they were criminals against humanity. And if they hadn't known and couldn't say NO, they were so morally retarded as to be unsalvageable as human beings. A child-molester is hunted down, sometimes by entire communities. Yet, the child-molester is only a threat to one child at a time. The children of Hiroshima were molested by men they never knew, men they never saw, men from whom they couldn't even run. These child-molesters, however, were not put into mental hospitals or jails. They were given raises, awards by community organizations, praise from the government and paragraphs in the history books.

The time had come for the youth to seize the responsibility for their own lives. The preparations for the future could not be entrusted to those who were responsible for the past. Indeed, it could be asked whether they should have been entrusted with the responsibility for their own lives, considering what they had done with them.

## HISTORY OF THE WORLD SINCE 1945

War in Indonesia (1945–47) between Netherlands and rebels

War in China (1945–49) between Nationalists and Communists

War in Kashmir (1947–49) between India and Pakistan

War in Greece (1946–49) between Government and ELAS rebels

War in Israel (1948–49) between Israel and Palestinians

War in Philippines (1948–52) between Government and the Huks

War in Indochina (1945–54) between France and the Vietminh

War in Malaya (1945–54) between Britain and the Communists

War in Korea (1950–53) between United States and North Korea and China

War in Formosa (1950–   ) between United States and Chinese Communists

War in Kenya (1952–53) between Britain and the Mau Mau

War in Sinai (1956) between Israel and Egypt

War in Suez (1956) between Great Britain, France and Egypt

War in Hungary (1956) between Russia and Hungary

War in Quemoy-Matsu (1954–58) between Chinese Nationalists and Chinese Communists

War in Lebanon (1958) between United States, Lebanon and rebels

War in Tibet (1950–59) between Tibet and China

War in Cyprus (1955–59) between Britain and EOKA rebels

War in Algeria (1956–62) between France and FLN

War in Cuba (1956–59) between Government and guerrillas

War in Laos (1959–   ) between Government and Pathet Lao

War in Kuwait (1961) between Britain and Iraq

War in Goa (1961) between India and Portugal

War in Yemen (1962–  ) between Royalists and Government, Egypt

War in Congo (1960–62) between Government, United Nations and secessionists and mercenaries

War in Cuba (1961) between United States and Cuba

War in South Vietnam (1952–  ) between United States and NLF

War in Himalayas (1959–62) between India and China

War in Angola (1960–  ) between Portugal and guerrillas

War in West New Guinea (1962) between Netherlands and Indonesia

War in Colombia (1960–  ) between Government and guerrillas

War in Cuba (1962) between Russia, Cuba and the United States

War in Algeria-Morocco (1963) between Algeria and Morocco

War in Venezuela (1963) between Government and guerrillas

War in Malaysia (1963–   ) between Britain, Malaysia and Indonesia

War in Congo (1964–  ) between Government and Simbas

War in Thailand (1964–   ) between Government and guerrillas

War in Dominican Republic (1965) between United States and Dominicans

War in Peru (1965–  ) between Government and guerrillas

War in Pakistan-India (1965) between Pakistan and India

Weariness makes this list incomplete, but the following wars of the late sixties can be added:

War in Bolivia between Government and guerrillas
War in Guatemala between Government and guerrillas
War in Mozambique between Portugal and FRELIMO
War in Southern Rhodesia between Government and African guerrillas
War in Portuguese Guinea between Portugal and PGAIC
War in Biafra between Biafra and Nigeria
War in Israel-Jordan-Syria between Israel and Arab states

# 2.

The sixth day of August in the Year of Our Lord nineteen hundred and forty-five. (Have mercy upon us.) Hiroshima. (Have mercy upon us, most merciful Father.)

> The run was short and straight.
> At 9:15 A.M.
> Major Thomas Ferebee

pressed the toggle
and the single bomb was away.
It took less than 60 seconds.
Then, the brilliant
morning
sunlight
was slashed
by a more brilliant
white flash.
The first atomic bomb
had been dropped.

(*Time*—August 20, 1945)

Hiroshima. The name itself cries. Hi-ro-shi-ma.

A single atomic bomb,
the first weapon of its type
ever used against a
target,
exploded over the city of Hiroshima
at 0815
on the morning of 6 August 1945.

Because of the lack of warning
and the populace's indifference
to small groups of planes,
the explosion came as an almost
complete surprise,
and the people
had not taken shelter.
Many were caught in the open,
and most of the rest
in flimsily constructed homes
or commercial establishments.

Seventy to eighty thousand people
were killed,

or missing
and presumed dead,
and an equal number
were injured.

(*The Effects of the Atomic Bomb at
Hiroshima and Nagasaki*—U.S.
Government Printing Office, 1946.)

No regrets were ever expressed. Instead, America has made it clear that, if necessary, there will be an encore. (Let there be one, two, three, many Hiroshimas.) All's fair in love and war. Particularly war.

(I was seven when the bomb was dropped. I don't remember it, however. Something should've interrupted the marble games and rock battles in broken-glass-Kansas City, Kansas-alleys to have made me remember that day from the others. Something should've happened. But it didn't.

I do remember the war, however. It drove down an Arkansas highway past Aunt Ada's house in khaki green trucks stuffed with khaki green dressed white men. Hour after hour it rolled by. It was there when I awoke in the hot summer morning and it was there when I said my prayers in the hot summer night. War was saving the keys from coffee cans and taking them to school. It was buying butter, all white in a plastic bag, and squeezing it until the little yellow globule in the center had spread throughout the whiteness and made it yellow. And there was the fight with some kid who talked about the "dirty Japs." They were Japanese, not Japs, and I fought him. The war was the vestibule of my father's church in Kansas City, where a plaque hung on which were listed the names of the men of the church who had been killed in the war. I was too young to put faces with the names, but I tried. I tried.)

August 6 is a day of mourning for the Japanese and Luci Baines Johnson Nugent's wedding anniversary. (Which side are you on?) On that day the world as it was previously known ended. The war was over (but only after another atomic bomb was dropped on Nagasaki) and Victory in Japan was hysterically celebrated. Enough had been killed. (And that's the way a war ends. That's the way a war ends.)

In Europe the war was over too, and it lay in nonradioactive rubble. No longer would good German citizens have to inhale the ashes of the dead. (How much coal did it take to keep the furnaces of Auschwitz and Belsen at the "right" temperature?)

### THE CITIZEN

Dr. Louis Frederick Fieser,
who led a team of Harvard University scientists
in the development of napalm
during World War II,
says
he feels
free
of
"any guilt."

"I was working
on a
technical problem
that was considered pressing."

"I distinguish between
developing a munition of some kind
and
using it,"
he declared.
"You can't blame the
outfit that put out the
rifle
that killed the President.
I'd do it again,
if called upon,
in defense of
the country."

"I don't know enough
about the
situation in
Vietnam,"
he said.
"It's not my
business
to deal with the
political
or
moral
questions.
That is a very involved thing.
Just because I played a role
in the technological development of
napalm
doesn't mean I'm any more qualified
to comment on the
moral
aspects of it."

(*The New York Times*—December 27, 1968)

The world should have been exhausted. Much of

it was in ruins and in some places the dead and near-dead outnumbered the living. The world should've taken a vacation. A long one. No world can absorb Hitler and the dropping of the atomic bomb and begin to recuperate in one generation. The world should've stopped and asked itself how it had allowed a Hitler to exist. It should've been so outraged at the dropping of the bomb that it would have refused to turn until everyone understood how the human soul had become so poisoned as to allow such to happen. Indeed, the world should have gone into a century of mourning for itself. It should have, but there was barely a pause to consider what had been done.

The forties tumbled into the fifties with the Berlin Airlift, a civil war in Greece, the coming to power of Mao Tse-tung (an event from which the U.S. has not yet recovered); and four years after V-J day, U.S. troops were in Asia once more. (It was the last Sunday in June and for some reason I had been awakened too late to read the paper before going off to Sunday School where Jesus Loved Me Yes I Knew although I was never sure why. I picked up the paper as I followed my parents out the door and there on the front page of the *Kansas City Star* was the headline: NORTH KOREAN REDS AT-TACK ROK. Beneath it was the picture of a tank.)

The United States was in Korea trying to stop the spread of communism in sub-zero cold and snow and after three years of fighting, what had changed? Communism had been stopped (Why?) and so had a lot of lives (in the cold, in the snow, in the long nights of eternal winters). Dwight David Eisenhower was elected President because he looked like everybody's grandfather (but not mine) and because he said he'd "Bring the boys home," home from the war of no victories and death (so red on the snow and ice).

World War II didn't end, but simply modulated around the circle of fifths with new variations. ("Let us not be deceived—we are in the midst of a cold war," Bernard Baruch announced in 1947.) The United States had the POWER to blackmail the world into peace (the silence of suffering humanity) and as long as it and no one else held that POWER, America had nothing to fear. But it wasn't long before Russia, a close ally of not too many years previous, announced that it, too, had the bomb. Run, John, run. Run to the laboratory, to the factory, to the uranium fields and build another. If they have one, we must have two. My God! They have two, too? Run, John, run. So it was, until one day there were enough nuclear weapons to blow up the world many times over. Man, once thought to be immortal (in his mortality) could be annihilated.

Having won the war, America felt that its just compensation should have been a world it controlled. Through the Marshall Plan, the occupation of Japan and foreign aid, the benevolent victors helped Europe and Asia rebuild (in the American way), thus fulfilling America's need for the world to be a mirror, reflecting America's image of itself as the highest exemplification of freedom in the history of Man. But in 1949, China joined Russia in the attempt at a new definition of Man and America felt threatened. Its leaders began speaking of the "Iron Curtain" and "the menace of Communism." People who had never been to communist countries wrote books about the "evils of Communism" and anti-Communism became the American way.

America found that it could not control the world it had won fair and square. Things would've been different if it hadn't been for the Communists. Not only those in Russia and China, but those who called themselves Americans and took their orders from the Kremlin.

### THE SCAPEGOATS

Julius
Rosenberg and his wife
were listening to the
*Lone Ranger*
with their two young sons
when
a stranger rapped
on the door of their drab apartment.
Twelve men filed in
from the small hallway
and announced that they were from the
FBI.
They arrested 32-year-old
Julius
Rosenberg as a spy.

(*Time*—July 31, 1950)

The Rosenbergs were electrocuted; the name Alger Hiss became the new American synonym for traitor. Morton Sobell went to jail and thousands more found themselves without jobs or friends during the hysteria of a Communist here, a Communist there, here a Communist, there a Communist, everywhere a Commie, Commie. When Joseph McCarthy declared that he had the names of Communists who were making policy in the State Department, America was pathetically ready to believe him. America had to believe him. And anyone who was not for the obliteration of Communists and Communism was *ipso facto* "soft," therefore dangerous, therefore guilty of treason by implication. Future leaders for peace and freedom and democracy, like Robert Kennedy, worked with McCarthy as he found the hammer and sickle in every library and on the lapel of any suit worn by an intellectual. It was enough for a man to be considered a Communist because he would not say he wasn't. But how can a man prove what he is not?

(Q. Sarah Good what evil spirit have you familiarity with?
A. None.
Q. Have you made no contracts with the devil?
Good answered no.
Q. What doe you hurt these children?
A. I doe not hurt them. I scorn it.
Q. Who doe you imploy then to doe it?
A. I employ no body.
Q. Have you made no contract with the devil?
A. No.
Q. Who doe you serve?
A. I serve God.
Q. What God doe you serve?

Her answers were in a very wicked spitfull manner, reflecting and retorting against the authority with base and abusive words and many lies shee was taken in. It was here said that her husband had said that he was afraid that she either was a witch or would be one very quickly. The worsh. Mr. Harthorn asked him his reason why he said so of her, whether he had ever seen anything by her, he answered no, not in this nature, but it was her bad carriage to him, and indeed said he I may say with tears the shee is an enemy to all good.

A death warrant was issued July 19, 1692, and Sarah Good was duly executed.)

(From *Profile of America* by Emily Davie.)

(And if a *man* cannot prove what he is not, weep, weep, for Sarah Good.)

The number of witches being hanged slowly diminished, but not because anyone had challenged and defeated the practice. Joe McCarthy simply proved to be an ineffective hangman. A few years later McCarthy died, but the hanging tree is still silhouetted in the moonlight.

It is unclear why those who were responsible didn't look at Joseph McCarthy and say, "Aw, man. Come off that shit." If it had not been for television and McCarthy's lack of Machiavellian finesse, he might have been president. But McCarthy killed himself during the thirty-six days of the televised Army-McCarthy hearings in 1954. Millions watched a balding lawyer from Boston look at the Senator and say quietly, "Have you no sense of decency, sir, at long last? Have you left no sense of decency?" If any one man destroyed McCarthy, it was this lawyer, Joseph Welch; and millions saw McCarthy's sickened grin in response to Welch's morality. Few, however, changed their minds concerning McCarthy. Television simply made it apparent that the man lacked the proper style.

# 3.

Television not only brought McCarthy into microscopic perspective for all to see, it gave the world a home in every house and America did not know how to cope with the guest who came for dinner and stayed. (There used to be another world, a world before Janie was born, a world in which my father and I listened to the baseball games on the radio. There were no crowd noises, no sound as the bat hit the ball, no yelling from the infield. Only the sound of a ticker-tape machine and a man's voice reading the action from the tape. It's two-and-two on Bauer in the top of the eighth." He would try to liven it up—"Here comes the pitch. Low and outside. Ball three!" But I knew that he'd made up the description of the action. It didn't matter. We sat at the kitchen table and listened to that ticker-tape machine and that voice and saw the game oh so vividly and it was real! World War II had been the voices of H. V. Kaltenborn and Edward R. Murrow. The next war would be grubby suppertime pictures of bombs dropping, huts burning and people dying in living color.) Out went the lights in the living room and the family sat for hours, watching, watching, watching. Their shadows were flung against the wall by the light from the set like shadows of Cro-Magnon Man sitting around a fire in his cave sometime after the Snake had done its deed. In Toledo, Ohio, the Water Commissioner discovered that water consumption rose fantastically during certain three minute periods. After many days of trying to find what had gone wrong in the city's water system, the answer finally came to him. The bladders and bowels of Toledo, Ohio, were now being suppressed until the commercials came on.

The American form of greeting became, "Did you see the Such-and-Such show last night?" A mass culture was created and if one answered the new form of greeting with "I don't have a TV set," he slowly found himself with little to say in which others were interested. Milton Berle, "I Love Lucy," Sid Caesar and Imogene Coca, Arthur Godfrey and others became the common referents and common experiences. American culture became synonymous with the fantasies of individuals whose profession is based upon fantasies, which are then sold to a sponsor who creates fantasies to make people think that the soap in the blue box gets clothes whiter than white while the soap in the orange box only gets them white. Add all the fantasies together and you get MONEY, the ultimate fantasy.

While the young girls of Hi-ro-shi-ma came to womanhood to find their wombs covered with the dust of 6 August 1945, Americans were exploring the joys of precooked, frozen foods. All that could not be frozen had been dehydrated, put into boxes and labeled INSTANT. Entire meals were cooked and frozen, put into aluminum containers that needed only to be placed in the oven and dinner was ready. They were called TV dinners.

While the young women of Hi-ro-shi-ma writhed and screamed in labor and gave birth to deformed children, American men discovered the breast. Jayne Mansfield, Marilyn Monroe, Sherry North and countless other platinum-covered (did they dye the pubic hair, too?) women found themselves famous for being a bigger piece of meat than some other women. *Playboy* magazine brought the middle-class male fantasy of Woman to national attention with its color fold-out of the Playmate of the Month, because that's what women are for—playing with. Other magazines followed with bigger breasts and bigger asses, with women lying on rugs, couches, beds, and rocks by the ocean, with their legs cocked at assorted, allegedly sexy, angles. Page after page and at lunchtime at magazine racks across the country, well-dressed, respectable-looking men stand solemnly in front of the racks, leafing slowly through the magazines, page after page, one magazine after another. They stand so no one can see if the well-pressed pants are beginning to bulge, but no one would look, because no one wants to know and no one ever looks anybody in the eye. They stand there, dreaming their dreams and at night, how many of them close their eyes, thrust themselves into their wives and in the ensuing minutes transform wives into the big-breasted, willing-hipped girls of the magazines? How many wives know that their husbands have never slept with them but merely used the availability of their bodies as the raw material for fantasies induced by a pose a photographer ordered a girl to take if she wanted to get paid. The sexual fantasies of men became big business, while any woman who admitted having sexual fantasies was a whore. A man named Kinsey came out with a study that said women like it. The book was a best seller (to men or women?). Never having been able to acknowledge that men and women were made of flesh, America began to broadcast the fact as if it were news.

The instant entertainment flowing simultaneously into millions of homes, the instant meals being heated at 350° (F) for twenty minutes (and serve), the purloined sex and guilty erections and the highest level of living in the world did not create a happier people. The adults, however, played their roles and smiled for 250th of a second at f.11.

The young didn't. They were called "The Silent Generation," but that was because no one was listening to their heartbeats. They were in the street dousing old men with kerosene and setting them afire, fighting each other with zip guns and Leonard Bernstein saw it all as a romantic *West Side Story* with pretty songs sung in beautifully rounded tenor and soprano tones. The more intellectual of the young (and it was always the quiet, bright student) practiced with their rifles until they were expert marksmen and then sent their parents into the Great Void. They knew that something was not right, as they were being served instantly. They knew, as they sat at the feet of their gray flanneled fathers, listening eagerly to the day's exciting tales of how two hundred extra cases of white thread were sold to a client who didn't need them. They knew, the teen-age girl on Mockingbird Lane in a suburb of a Texas city whose father did nothing but work, come home, watch TV and drink beer before going to bed to do it all again the next day. She knew and one day she stayed home from school to kill her family, because she was "tired of seeing them suffer." They knew. The young always do and they protested, but no one understood. The fathers and the mothers offered many answers, the old answers, and the sociologists filled the magazines with articles on juvenile delinquency and Billy Graham, Norman Vincent Peale and Fulton Sheen gave the old answers a new twist and preached that a return to God meant higher profits. (Of course God is dead. The pistol still smokes in our hands.)

Those who were not in the streets, on the corners, back in the alleys, at the drive-ins, were in their rooms, watching, waiting, looking, knowing that when they could see a way out of the homes where the sounds from the TV smashed all possibility of thought and feeling, when they could get the slightest intimation vibration adumbration of an alternative to following in Dad's footsteps out the back door and into the garage every morning at 7:30, they would take it. All roads lead to a time clock, the teachers, preachers, parents said, with know-it-all smiles. The children said nothing, but late at night, in the quiet of their rooms, when the television sets were silent, they prepared themselves. For what, they didn't know. But when it came, they would recognize it, as a Mississippi farmer recognizes which rain of spring is the last one, and the cotton seeds can be planted without fear of their being washed away. (There was a day, a hot Nashville summer day. I was seventeen, riding on the bus, the back of the bus. In my hand was the second issue of *Evergreen Review*. How it had gotten there, down to me, black me, in Nashville, I don't remember. But I had it in my hand, turning the pages slowly, understanding nothing of what passed before my eyes. And then: "I saw the best minds of my generation destroyed by madness,/starving hysterical naked,/dragging themselves through the negro streets at dawn look-/ing for an angry fix." I closed the book, not knowing what it said, what it meant or where it had come from, but the long nights of waiting were over. There was another day, an afternoon, a September afternoon of the same year when I walked in Otey's Grocery at 18th and Jefferson and picked up a copy of *Esquire* magazine and started browsing through it. The first article was by somebody named John Clellon Holmes called "The Philosophy of the Beat Generation." My eyes focused on those words, "Beat Generation," and I saw myself. Hastily I scanned the article until I read, "Everyone who has lived through a war, any sort of war, knows that beat means, not so much weariness, as rawness of the nerves; not so much being 'filled up to here,' as being emptied out. It describes a state of mind from which all unessentials have been stripped, leaving it receptive to everything around it, but impatient with trivial obstructions." I closed the magazine, bought it and smiled. Everyone could see the copy of the magazine in my hand. What they could not see was the self growing inside me.)

Those who came to be known as the Beat Generation had barely entered their twenties when the world changed at Hiroshima. They had been at that

most exciting of ages, the early twenties, when you
feel life stretching before you, waiting for you to
impress your image upon its fictile face. But the
world had no face after Hiroshima. It bled from
every pore and those in their neonatal womanhood
and manhood set themselves the task of stanching
the rivulets of blood pouring from the soul of Man.
The pain of Hiroshima, the grim winters of Korea
and the shadow of the hanging tree stretched across
America. That was what their lives were supposed
to affirm and they refused. Like those who killed
their parents while they slept, the Beat Generation
saw no reason to accept the values America presented them on the commuter trains leaving Grand
Central Station, filled with the men in the gray
flannel suits and V.I.P. cases, passing through Harlem with their eyes on the closing stock market
quotations. (One day the train won't make it out
of Harlem and the stock market will not reopen
when the sun rises the next day.) So they dropped
out and Jack Kerouac described them On The Road
hitchhiking back and forth from San Francisco to
Denver to New Orleans to New York and back
"angel-headed hipster high," smoking pot, listening
to jazz, reading Zen, "Plotinus Poe St. John of the
Cross" and writing haiku on bus station walls in
Pittsburgh. They dropped out and grew beards, let
their hair hang low and the women dressed in black
sweaters, skirts, leotards. They created their own
society, where they lived, worked, talked, loved and
presented a visible alternative to those still in the
loneliness of adolescent rooms. There was a way out
for those imprisoned in states of mind called Nashville, Dayton, Palmyra, Salt Lake City, Topeka,

Worcester. Catatonia was not the only alternative to psychosis. While Fidel liberated the Sierra Maestras, the Beat Generation created a liberated zone on North Beach in San Francisco. In their liberation, they thought of themselves as "white Negroes," rejects from society, outsiders, and they listened to jazz and got high and romanticized what they thought were the lives of black people.

(June 13, 1959
7 P.M.

Talk about tired! I've been hunting for a place all day and one possibility. The most disgusting thing is that most people seem to read the sign that flashes over my head. It flashes so bright that soon it'll be inside of me and this'll make me bitter, which I don't want. Went in one place and got the proverbial, "Somebody just took it. Just hadn't had time to take the sign down." The lie was too obvious. If I'd been thinking, I would've gone to the window and politely removed the sign. The amazement on his face when I entered said quite loudly, "What th' hell is this nigger doing in here?"

Well, I'm sitting in one of the North Beach places now. When I first hit this part of town I wanted to laugh. The people are so ludicrous. The first thing that occurred to me was, what is their motivation? And all the Negroes! But it's no wonder. Here at least you're accepted, but it's more because you're a Negro and not so much as an individual. I want to be accepted as plain ol' me and rejected on the same basis. But it's a little better to be accepted because you are a Negro rather than rejected for the same reason.

I would like to get an apartment over here, but price will probably eliminate me. But North Beach is nice with its narrow streets and hidden alleys. Also it's near the Bay and you know my passion for water.

The characters that stroll in and out. Long hair, beards—do you take them seriously? They seem to me to be bums masquerading under the banner of the avant-garde. This is all like watching something on the stage.

The "beatnik" attitude toward the Negro is interesting, because it creates a new Negro. America's born Outsider can now belong. He who accepted before his position of unacceptance in society, now is made to know consciously that he is oppressed. "But we accept you. We, the beatniks are white Negroes. We are emulating your reaction to society." So now the Negro is a paragon of sorts, and what develops is a new Uncle Tom. Not the obsequious old man down South, but a "balling fool" who can ball and be praised for it.

In the South you accept segregation as a granite fact, but here it's more subtle, more cruel. In Nashville, white people looked at me, called me a nigger and frowned. Here they look at me, call me a nigger and want to hug me. Either way *I* end up being nonexistent.)

The new selves the Beat Generation created appeared insincere only because they did not yet fit comfortably. But with their thirst to live, with their intensity to feel everything (FEEL) as if no one had ever ever ever ever felt before, they were real. Henry Miller and Rimbaud became minor saints because they had the same hungry intensity, the desire to rearrange derange the senses, so they might know more, feel more and above all, be more. Being was all. Don't be good; don't be evil. They were religious fanatics seeking union with God. Not the God of Our Father who art in Heaven (and what're YOU doing up there when the mess is down here), but the God that walked the streets and lay in the sun and all manner of good emanated from His BEING.

Being. To Be. In America one was taught TO DO. (The kitchen. That's where I always had the most serious talks with my mother. While she was cooking. "I think I want to be a monk," I told her one afternoon. "A monk?" she exclaimed with horror. "Why?" "Well, that's the only way I could devote all my time to God." "But, Julius. Monks don't *do* anything.") But what one did affected one's Be-ing and to correct that, Western society evolved Freud, and countless other systems of psychiatry that adjust one's Being so that you can continue the Doing. The society depended upon people Doing and if they suddenly wanted TO BE, the society would disintegrate. If people cared more about the man who wore the clothes than the clothes on the man, fortunes would disappear in a matter of minutes.

The Beat Generation cared enough to kill within themselves a lifetime of being educated to do. They cared enough to hold a small protest demonstration in downtown San Francisco on 6 August 1959. (It had never occurred to me to protest the bombing of Hiroshima. I would observe the day in my introverted way, but I didn't know one could do anything else. Only a few of them protested, but it was a small reminder that radioactive matter was still falling from the explosion of that August morning and that it would continue to fall until something, something happened. But none of us knew what.) They cared enough to sit for hours and talk about other ways. Most of them believed in nonviolence, even when the police beat and arrested the black poet Bob Kaufman. ("Well, I see where a white jury down South sentenced a white guy to the electric chair for the rape of a Negro girl," someone said to me one day sarcastically. "Oh yeah!" I exclaimed. "Yeah. I guess that's real equality. Instead of abolishing capital punishment, spread it around." I didn't respond, because there was nothing to say. Maybe he was right, but retribution was retribution and it was long overdue. To take a life was wrong, but I couldn't help being happy thinking about that cracker sitting in the electric chair.)

They were real and America regarded them as freaks. The photographers came to North Beach with their Nikons; the reporters with their built-in-answer questions ("What do you think your parents would think if they could see you now?"). On weekends, the tourist buses drove slowly up North Beach's Grant Street; the soldiers and sailors on weekend passes came, got drunk and lined the sidewalk, yelling, "You need a bath!" "The Army barber should get his hands on you!" And Allen Ginsberg left for India; Gary Snyder went to Japan; Kerouac took to the road once more and ended up at his mother's on Long Island; John Clellon Holmes bought a house in Connecticut; Pierre de Lattre, the priest of the Bread and Wine Mission (whose wife always looked so unhappy), disappeared and others vanished into the wilds of Big Sur, the sewage waste of Venice West and to various other asylums in the outer circles of respectability, while Bill Margolis jumped off the roof and was paralyzed forever and Bob Kaufman's wife Eileen, who must be close to forty now, can be seen walking through Washington Square Park in New York on spring afternoons, smiling to herself, pushing their child in a stroller, a creature from another world, another time, and all those around her think she's only a housewife out with her kid for the day.

The stream did not die. It made its way underground and the black dress of the women (the faces pale with no make-up) became a uniform for a generation of college students. Beards and sandals became the language of new states of mind.

America quickly assimilated the first post-Hiroshima rebellion. It absorbed what the Beat Generation offered culturally—the influx of Japanese and Eastern culture, a new dynamism in poetry and prose, and fashions—and rang it up on the cash register. Others, however, internalized the truths the Beat Generation had brought and resolved to continue the journey.

# 4.

Across the tracks in Afroamerica, the talk was of integration. To the white male southern mind it sounded too much like intercourse and if there was anything which drove a cracker over the brink of insanity it was the thought of a big, black dick sliding in and out of a white pussy. (What the white female mind thought of the idea has not been recorded in the annals of history. And the white man is afraid for it to be.) In Afroamerica, however, integration had little to do with the white man's nightmares. It was simply the black way of saying don't tell me where I can and can't go. As long as white society restricted the movements of blacks, it deprived blacks of that basic right to decide for themselves. To the white supremacist mind, that was too subtle. Blacks wanted to go to white schools because white people were better, whites thought. Blacks had to go to white schools, so they could eventually *choose* to go to black schools. But blacks couldn't articulate that in 1954. They wanted integration if for no other reason than because whites didn't want it. (It was a spring Monday afternoon and Nashville had already drifted into its warm weather lassitude which, by July, would become burdensome. I had meandered home from school and with nothing else to do, sat in the kitchen talking with mother while she fixed supper. When

I heard the evening paper hit the front porch, I went to get it. I unrolled the paper, stared at the headline and smiled.

"Momma," I said, walking into the kitchen. "Guess what?"

"Hm?"

"I'm going to Hume-Fogg in September." Hume-Fogg was the only commercial high school in Nashville. It was all white and I wanted to study commercial art, because I thought it would be an enjoyable way to earn a living. But commercial art wasn't taught at Pearl High, the black school.

"Boy, what're you talking about?"

I held up the paper for her to see the headline. She frowned. "What do you want to go there for?"

I laughed. "To make the white folks mad."

But I finished high school, college, and moved to New York and Hume-Fogg was still all-white.)

Integration. The Supreme Court had spoken and for the first time within the memory of young blacks, there was a sign of hope. Segregation was not eternal. God was on our side. (That summer I sat down beside white people on the bus, or sat in the white section, just to make white people mad, to let them know that the Supreme Court would back me up if they started trouble. I started going to white parks, just to let them know that we were now on the scene.)

### HEROINE

On Dec. 1, 1955
Mrs. Rosa Parks, a 42-year-old Negro seamstress, was ordered by a Montgomery City Lines bus driver

to get up and make way for
some white passengers.
She refused,
was arrested
and fined $10.

(*Time*—January 16, 1956)

The blacks of Montgomery decided that if Mrs.
Parks couldn't ride the bus in peace, then no blacks
would ride until all could ride in peace. For months
they walked. When asked if she weren't getting tired
of walking, one old sister said: "My soul has been
tired for a long time. Now my feet are tired and
my soul is resting." (The people are the true poets.
The rest of us, with our advances and royalty
checks, are just journeymen making a dishonest
living.)

From that confrontation in Montgomery came a
man whose face, canorous voice and graphic words
became symbols for the first phase of the black
struggle. "This is not a tension between the Negroes
and whites," the then twenty-seven-year-old Martin
Luther King, Jr., said. "This is only a conflict between justice and injustice. We are not just trying
to improve the whole of Montgomery. If we are arrested every day; if we are exploited every day; if
we are triumphed over every day; let nobody pull
you so low as to hate them."

Whites didn't mind being loved, but that didn't
mean they were going to allow blacks to go to school
with their children. (If niggers ain't got tails, you
still got to watch out for them long black dicks.)
Mansfield, Texas; Clinton, Tennessee; Sturgis and
Clay, Kentucky, were the sites in 1956 of white

resistance to the Supreme Court ruling and a year later came Little Rock. Nine black children walked through a mob of howling maniacs who had multiple orgasms spitting, kicking, beating, chasing, cursing the nine children. The Supreme Court had spoken and that was supposed to be the law of the land. Eventually, troops were sent to Little Rock, but it was too late for many young blacks. (I remember the face of only one of those children. She was pretty and when I saw her picture in the paper, I wanted to be there beside her. It was hard for me to live with myself if I couldn't at least suffer with her. Her name was Elizabeth Eckford and they made her cry. I was eighteen then and I knew that they would have to pay for making her cry. If nothing else had ever happened, that was enough. Someday. Somewhere. They would pay.)

As blacks organized bus boycotts in Tallahassee, Florida, lunch counter sit-ins in Oklahoma City, Oklahoma, the Russians sent a satellite orbiting around the earth, and the night sky became an object of terror. (A few of us cheered Sputnik. Anybody who could beat this country at something was all right with us. One girl on the campus of Fisk University even sent a telegram of congratulations to the Kremlin. I would mention her name, as I thought that was a heroic act, but she's now working for the State Department and might not want folks to know what she was like when she was a freshman in college.) Because the Russians were able to put a satellite into space first, Americans wondered if it meant that communism was superior to democracy. Articles appeared comparing the Russian system of education to America's and it was discovered that Johnny couldn't read and Ivan could. (But the United States had a higher GNP.)

The world outside helped to intensify the contradictions between America and Afroamerica. Black people watched with little interest the television films of Hungarians throwing bricks at Russian tanks. There was no need to take sides, because neither represented anything with which blacks could identify. But when the United States opened wide its doors and rolled out the red carpet for the Hungarian refugees, Afroamerica was acutely aware that the only carpet leading from its doors to America was filled with tacks sticking straight up in the air and the rules of the game stated that you had to walk it barefooted. (San Diego, Calif. The winter of 1959. For the first time in my twenty years, I found myself living physically where I was outnumbered and it was frightening. White people. White people. Everywhere. In my classes at San Diego State College, I was the only black in each class. One afternoon leaving school, a white teacher offered me a ride. I accepted and as I settled in the car, he turned slightly to introduce the person sitting beside him. "Julius. I want you to meet one of our Hungarian friends." Once again and yet once again, the four hundred years of my life did not exist in the mind of a white person. If they had, then he would've known no Hungarian refugee was a friend of mine. No Hungarian refugee could ever be a friend of mine until I, too, could walk on the red carpet. The Hungarian turned around and said a heavily-accented "Hello." I made a sound which could've been interpreted as civil and tried to stop the pain of not existing in the eyes of white people except as they wanted me to exist. When I slept in class, I was the bright young colored boy, who obviously had to work nights to support his family, come home and study, and go to school the next day. Thus one teacher rationalized my sleeping through his boring class and even went so far as to announce one day that he understood and it was all right if I slept in his class. When I was introduced to the Hungarian, I was a red, white and blue American. I've been waiting ever since for the Russians to go into Hungary again and really kick some ass.)

As the decade came to a close, a giant of a man came out of the mountains of Cuba. Fidel Castro caused the United States little worry at first. Those Latins were always changing governments every few months anyway. Slowly, however, the United States began realizing that this was a little different, as Castro took over the U.S.-owned sugar fields, plantations and industries. Fidel was not Batista by another name. Fidel was Fidel and he was only ninety miles away.

## MAY 4, 1959

Shortly past midnight
a group of about
eight or ten dark figures
darted through the moonlight
toward the Poplarville, Miss., courthouse.
Opening a window,
they slipped into the sheriff's office.
They seemed to know that
the jailer was gone
for the night.

They knew, too,
that the cell keys
were in a metal cabinet
in the sheriff's office.
Wearing gloves and masks,
some of them pushed their way into the cell area.

Mack Charles Parker,
23,
a truck driver scheduled to go on
trial
for
the
rape
of a 24-year-old white woman,
leaped from his bunk,
pulled on his pants,
made for the shower.
For a moment
the men fumbled with the key,
then opened the cell door
and rushed in.
"Get him! Get him!"
one man snarled.
They swarmed all over him.

"I didn't do it,"
Parker screamed.
"I didn't do it!
"Don't let 'em do me like this!
"Help me!"

One of the intruders
began bludgeoning Parker
with a pistol,
another with a stick.
A third picked up a garbage can
and hit him.

Parker went down,
bleeding.
Down the concrete steps
they dragged him,
feet first,
his head cracking again
and again
on the treads.
Blood trailed the figures
as they stumbled onward,
and a
bloody handprint
was slapped on the doorstep.

The other prisoners ran to the window,
saw the men fling
their victim into a car,
watched as the car
and four or five other autos
drove off.

Parker's terror-choked voice
was drowned by the chatter of youngsters
leaving a dance
down the street.

(*Time*—May 4, 1959)

On the first day of the second month of the sixth decade of the twentieth century four black students sat down at a dime store lunch counter in Greensboro, North Carolina. The era of confrontation had begun. The chickens were coming home to roost— not by ones, not by twos, but by tens.

# two

# 1.

February 1. By February 10, the sit-ins had spread
to fifteen cities in five southern states. By September of 1961, there had been demonstrations in more
than one hundred cities in twenty states. Seventy
thousand students, practically all of them black, had
demonstrated against segregated institutions. Some
thirty-six hundred of them had been arrested.

(There was little excitement on the campus of
Fisk University the evening of February 1 when
we first got the news about the sit-in at Greensboro.
Four guys had gone into a dime store, sat at the
lunch counter and asked to be served. They were
refused    and    subsequently    arrested    when    they

wouldn't leave. Since the previous fall some students at Fisk had been talking about doing something similar. They had had several meetings with the managers of various dime stores about desegregating their lunch counters, and had been turned down, of course. I had been asked to go to these meetings. "What th' hell I want to sit beside a white person and drink coffee for?" had been my response. I was a senior and knew that once I graduated I was going to shake not only the dust of the South from my shoes, but that of America as well. I was going to go to New York and work for a year and then cut out for England and hang it up. The lunch counters could stay segregated forever as far as I was concerned.)

The first mass arrests of the sixties occurred in Nashville on the last Saturday of February. (Every time there was a demonstration that month it had snowed. That Saturday it didn't and everybody who went to sit-in that day knew that they would probably be arrested. I'd had a date with Candy for that night and was a little pissed when I heard she had been among the seventy-eight arrested. I never got another chance to go out with her, either, because those who were sitting-in became an "in" group and a rather incestuous one. I sure wanted to hit on her, but no woman was worth risking a beating and jail.)

Like a fire leaping from one room to another until the entire house is consumed, the young of the world came out of their rooms and their parents did not recognize them. In England, thousands marched from Aldermaston to London to protest nuclear weapons. South Korean and Turkish youth took to the streets in demonstrations which led to the fall of the governments in both countries. Fifty-six were killed during a demonstration in Sharpesville, South Africa, and on December 20, 1960, those who had been organizing and conducting nonviolent demonstrations against the regime of Ngo Dinh Diem in South Vietnam organized the National Liberation Front, resolving that there was no other way except the gun.

In the summer of 1961, the sit-in movement gave way to the Freedom Rides. Thirteen members of the Congress of Racial Equality (CORE) boarded a bus in Washington, D.C. Their destination was New Orleans, Louisiana. They wanted to test a recent Supreme Court decision, which said that no passenger engaged in interstate travel could be subjected to segregated facilities in bus terminals or segregated seating aboard the buses. The Supreme Court could say what it wanted, but the Freedom Rides made it clear (to the blind) that the South would do as it wanted. The Freedom Riders were beaten in Rock Hill, S.C., arrested in Winnsboro, S.C., beaten outside of Anniston, Ala., and almost killed by a lead-pipe-carrying mob in the bus station at Birmingham. The original thirteen could go no farther. Veterans of the Nashville sit-in movement decided that the Freedom Rides had to continue. They went to Birmingham and boarded a bus for Montgomery, Ala., where they, in turn, were almost killed. (It was a Sunday morning when I read of the beatings in the paper. I remember looking at the picture of Jim Zwerg, a white student at Fisk, leaning against a wall, his face so bloody it was sickening to look at. I felt impotent and frustrated and the only recourse I had was to go into the streets with a gun and start killing white people. Instead, I went over to Fisk's campus to hang out for a while and to talk about what had happened.

"Did you hear about what happened to Jim?" I asked Marvin, the first person I saw.

"Naw, man. What happened?"

"He got beat up on the Freedom Rides."

There was a pause. "Oh yeah. What Freedom Rides, man?"

"You don't know about the Freedom Rides?"

"Naw, man. I been studying hard, you know."

I walked away without answering. A few years later when I learned that Marvin had been killed in Vietnam I could only consider it poetic justice.)

The beatings in Montgomery didn't stop the Freedom Rides, however. The Nashville students, joined now by Dr. King, decided to continue to New Orleans. (They never made it past Jackson, Miss., where they and all subsequent Freedom Riders were taken from the buses to the state prison.) Attorney General Robert Kennedy called Dr. King and asked for a cooling-off period and proved that he didn't understand. He should've told the crackers of Alabama, Mississippi, Georgia, etc., to take a cooling-off period, like two thousand years. After all, black people weren't fighting for something they shouldn't have had (were they?).

The manner in which the Kennedys tried to handle the Freedom Rides demonstrated that any differences between them and other politicians were only a matter of style. "Ask not what your country can do for you; ask what you can do for your coun-

try," John F. Kennedy had intoned at his inaugura-
tion. Those were the words of a young man who
was going to bring the country to the borders of
the New Frontier. They were challenging words and
the Kennedys and their extended family were people
who seemed capable of any challenge. With John
Kennedy in the White House and Jackie on the
front pages looking like the mistress of the hunt,
the country entered a period which was beyond an
intellectual's wildest dreams. Ideas were not only
listened to, but sought out. If brains could've glit-
tered like Christmas tree lights, then Washington
under the Kennedys was one continual December
25. The Kennedys gave the intellectual a place in
the smog-obscured sun and created an image with
which the young could identify. With their games
of touch football, their ability to laugh at themselves, their directness and honesty (?), they created a feeling of hope in most sectors of the nation.
(But it was John Kennedy who put Lyndon Johnson in the position where he could become President,
which he did.) They could be moved by the sight of
a miner's shack in West Virginia, by nigger-filled
ghetto streets. The Kennedys cared, we were told.
"Some men see things as they are and say why,"
Robert Kennedy said many times. "I dream things
that never were and say why not." They represented
hope to many who had ceased to hope. The Kennedys seemed to be aware that America had been
unable to make real the moral principles it articu-
lated. To pledge allegiance to a flag with liberty and
justice for all and have more than eleven per cent
of the population excluded from that is a contradiction which will sink any society (if the society

does not sink the eleven per cent). The Kennedys were going to resolve the contradiction. When Robert Kennedy asked the Freedom Riders to slow down, he only heightened that contradiction.

Throughout the summer of 1962, from California to the New York islands, blacks and whites boarded buses for Jackson, Miss., where they were immediately arrested and sent to serve thirty to sixty days. The Freedom Rides forced the federal government, through the Interstate Commerce Commission, to issue a ruling backing the Supreme Court's ruling. Because the government had refused to act in the initial phases of the Freedom Rides, it was clear that government under God and the Kennedys hadn't changed. The young wanted the government to act against injustices because the injustices existed. As always, the government acted because it was forced to.

1961

January
U.S. breaks relations with Cuba.

February
U.S. bans travel to Cuba.
Lumumba murdered in Congo. U.S. implicated.
Negroes demonstrate in U.N. gallery.

March
Kennedy sets

Two camps were established in the fifties from which the young would leave for their assaults upon the American Way of Life in the sixties. The first camp had been set up during the Montgomery bus boycotts. Demonstrations by the community replaced secret meetings between black leaders with the white power structure. The streets became the conference room and black leaders were forced to be responsive to the feelings and attitudes of the community, not the power structure.

up Peace Corps
and draws some
students from
"the movement."

April
Eichmann goes
on trial.
U.S. invades
Cuba.

May
Freedom Rides
start.

August
SNCC goes
into Miss.

September
Robert Will-
iams flees
country.
Herbert Lee
murdered in
Miss.

November
Women's Strike
for Peace or-
ganized.
3,000 City College
students in
N.Y.C. boycott
classes to pro-
test ban on
Communist speak-
ers.

1962

January
250 students
arrested at
Southern Univ.

The second camp, inaugurated by the Beat Generation, was the base for assaults upon America's values by white youth. The new generation wanted America to live its words, but the contradictions between America's deeds and its preachments would lead God Himself to the brink of insanity. It was a society concerned with buying and selling and a man's worth was measured by what he earned and what he owned. "Their basic problem is that they took American ethical words and preachments too seriously," said Dr. Kenneth Clark, a Negro (a subgroup of the black race) sociologist. That is something no one should be foolish enough to do.

## THE HUSTLER

It seems that
Paul Revere
may have made his
famous midnight ride for
money
as well as
patriotism.

Thomas Stotler,
40 years old,
a historian,
says he has a
document
in which

in Louisiana. Protests close school.

**February**
5,000 students march on Washington to protest war.

**June**
SDS issues Port Huron statement.

**Summer**
More than 1,000 arrested in civil rights demonstrations in Albany, Ga.

**September**
Miners organize in Hazard, Ky. White youth go to help.

**October**
James Meredith enters Univ. of Miss. Kennedy calls out troops. H. Stuart Hughes runs for Senate in Mass., on peace platform.

Revere listed an expense of 15 pounds six shillings for "riding for the Committee of Safety" in April and May, 1775.

"This certainly does not mean Revere wasn't a patriot,"
Mr. Stotler says.
"It just puts him in perspective.
Paul Revere didn't live on his horse, wide-eyed, waiting to race about the countryside. He had to work, like the rest of us, to feed his family."

(*The New York Times*— November 19, 1967)

The young could see little wrong with living on one's horse, "wide-eyed." Perhaps that was the only good. If an adult asked them, "What do you do?" they would have liked to respond, "I live." But the expected response is a definition: "I am an engineer." "I am a teacher." "I am a writer." When man is defined by how he earns his money, then man is no longer Man. He is merely an earning machine and the young had grown up observing such machines, though they were called (by the manufacturer?) Mommy and Daddy. Parents spent their lives acquiring chrome and glitter and a bigger and better and the ultimate reward came when the neighbors said that yes, yours is chromier and glitterier and better and it's worth every penny.

## THE CONSTITUTION

We own half the trucks
in the world.
We own almost half of all the radios
in the world.
We own a third of all the electricity that's produced
in the world.

And although we have only about
six per cent of the population
in the world,
we have half
of its wealth.
And bear in mind that other
94 per cent of the population
all would like to trade with us.

Now I would like to see them
enjoy the blessings
that we enjoy.
But don't you help them
exchange places with us
because
I don't want
to be
where they are.

(Speech by President Lyndon Johnson
to the Jr. Chamber of
Commerce—June 28, 1967)

Lyndon Johnson was proud of America's accomplishments. The young were ashamed of them and some considered these accomplishments to be the problem. Being six per cent of the world and owning half of its wealth (a modest figure) meant that more than half of the world had nothing. It was an impossible fact to live with.

We are people of this generation, bred in at least modest comfort, housed now in universities, looking uncomfortably to the world we inherit.

When we were kids the United States was the wealthiest and strongest country in the world; the only one with the atom bomb, the least scarred by modern war, an initiator of the United Nations that we thought would distribute Western influence throughout the world. Freedom and equality for each individual, government of, by, and for the people—these American values we found good, principles by which we could live as men. Many of us began maturing in complacency.

As we grew, however, our comfort was penetrated by events too troubling to dismiss. First, the permeating and victimizing fact of human degradation symbolized by the Southern struggle against racial bigotry, compelled most of us from silence to activism. Second, the enclosing fact of the Cold War, symbolized by the presence of the Bomb, brought awareness that we ourselves, and our friends, and millions of abstract "others" . . . might die at any time. We might deliberately ignore, or avoid, or fail to feel all other human problems, but not these two, for these were too immediate and crushing in their impact, too challenging in the demand that we as individuals take the responsibility for encounter and resolution. . . .

Our work is guided by the sense that we may be the last generation in the experiment with living . . .

(Port Huron Statement of the Students for a Democratic Society, 1962.)

They began a painful search for values and one of the first places they found any indication of another reality was in the music of poor blacks and poor whites. It was categorized as "folk music," meaning that it was legitimate for purposes of academic study, but not relevant to living. To the young, it was quite relevant. They could listen to this music, get out of themselves and into another place and time, where there was meaning and feeling. In those old songs sung by old people, there was a world, easily grasped and easily held. They went to Newport, Rhode Island, for folk festivals where they sat at the feet of men and women with such names as Mississippi John Hurt, Lightnin' Hopkins, Almeda Riddle, Son House, Skip James, Libba Cotton, and Doc Watson. They came with their guitars and banjos and mouth harps and autoharps and tried to play and sing like the old people. Being young and white wasn't good enough any more. In fact, it was becoming a liability. (It was rush hour when I got off the Greyhound bus. With guitar in one hand and suitcase in the other I walked outside to take my first look at New York City. For ten minutes I stood on the sidewalk looking at all the cars and all the people and wondered, what am I doing here? I was twenty-two years old, rumored to be a man, but I wanted nothing more than to be back in Nashville. I turned and went back in the station to get my nerves together. I had to. I didn't have the $25 to take a bus back to Nashville.

A young white boy, guitar case in one hand, girl holding the other, came up to me. "Let's play some," he said, putting his guitar case down and opening it. I looked at him. I wasn't particular about playing in the bus station, and breathed a sigh of relief when I saw a policeman approaching. The kid asked the cop, "Is there a law against playing the guitar?" He went on about how it was a free country and this was a democracy and before I knew it, I found myself standing outside trying to hail a cab. Maybe that white kid didn't know anything about democracy, but I knew that the gun hanging on the cop's waist defined freedom and I wasn't ready to quarrel with the dictionary.

Later I went down to Washington Square with what I thought was a guitar. It was little more than a varnished orange crate next to a Martin Dreadnought and I was intimidated and confused as I heard them (white!) singing about God's Gonna Trouble The Water and their Trouble In Mind and they bobbed their heads and bounced up and down in what I presumed they considered rhythm. What did they know of these songs we would sing in church and in the field, songs the old folks sang when they were ironing or just settin' on the porch in the evening as the sun went down and the frogs came out? Nobody had ever hated them. And who was this Joan Baez talking about all her trials would soon be over? The bitch was white, wasn't she? Plus, she was good-looking and was making money. The only kind of trials she could have had was deciding whether she should fly first-class or tourist.)

But if you were white (God forbid!) and you didn't like what that meant, you struck out through the forest, looking for paths, traces of paths or simply plunged into the brush and made your own. Blacks have always served as a path which whites have used to try and get out of the concentration camps of their souls. Whites are loath to admit that black people serve as therapy for them, but they have frantically imitated black music, dance, speech and dress in every year of every decade. If a black man says this, the white response is that this is merely replacing white racism and white superiority with black racism and black superiority. Notwithstanding, it is past time to say the obvious: Black culture is superior to white culture. (Read the sentence again. No one said that black people are superior to white people, or that John Coltrane is superior to Bach. If any white person wants to read racist overtones into that, that is his misfortune.) From the way whites have always used black culture as a means of getting out of themselves, the effeteness of white culture should be apparent. (And the fecundity of black culture. But I, a black man, cannot say that without being accused of a built-in inability to be disinterested and objective. That's why America prefers the history of slavery as told by the descendants of slave owners rather than a history told by the descendants of slaves.) Since white folks don't believe anything until it comes from white folks, listen to a white folk: "The cultural aggression of white America against Negroes and Indians is not based on skin color and belief in racial superiority, whatever ideological clothing may be used to rationalize it, but on the white man's inchoate awareness that the Negro and Indian—as men with deep roots in the resonating echo chamber of the discontinuous, interrelated tribal world—are actually psychically and socially superior to the fragmented, alienated and dissociated man of Western civilization. Such a recognition, which stabs at the heart of the white man's entire social value system, inevitably generates violence and genocide. It has been the sad fate of the Negro and the Indian to be tribal men in a fragmented culture—men born ahead of rather than behind their time." (Marshall McLuhan, *Playboy*—March, 1969.)

It was also logical that whites involved themselves in the civil rights movement, picketing Woolworth stores in the North while blacks sat-in at Woolworth's in the South. With the Freedom Rides, young whites also boarded buses to Mississippi, were arrested and went to jail. By 1963, a small group of them were working with blacks to organize demonstrations and freedom organizations in Mississippi, Georgia, and other southern states. They went because they felt guilty about the inertia of their parents. They went to save themselves from a world that gave them questions and no answers, but Daddy would take out a twenty dollar bill and say, go buy one. They went and in black society found a world in which they could feel human. They didn't realize that they were merely repeating the "white Negro" romanticism of the Beat Generation on another level. They could never be a part of the black community, no matter how hard they tried, no matter how many blacks they had as friends. Yet, there was no other way they could begin.

Nineteen sixty-three was the pivotal year for the civil rights movement and

1963

April

William Moore, a white postman, murdered while walking an Ala. highway, carrying a sign that read "Eat At Joe's— Black and White." Harvard fires Dr. Timothy Leary for giving LSD to students. Pope John XXIII issues "Pacem in Terris" encyclical.

for many of the young (who were aging rapidly) involved in it. There were more than ten thousand demonstrations that year and some five thousand blacks were arrested. Cambridge, Maryland; Danville, Virginia; and Birmingham, Alabama, were the sites of the principal battles. Gloria Richardson led the demonstrations in Cambridge and white resistance was so fierce, Cambridge was occupied for several months by the National Guard. ("Cambridge? Man, I never will forget Cambridge! Carmichael got gassed so bad he thought he was gon' die, jim. Yeah, and Cambridge was where Cliff Vaughs got bayoneted, too. Didn't teach the nigger no sense, though.") Cambridge eventually settled down to a state of quiet guerrilla warfare which still continues. Danville, Virginia, was a place of sadistic bloodletting. Demonstrators were beaten into blind alleys where other policemen waited with clubs and cattle prods to beat them into insensibility. Memories of Danville still cause civil rights veterans to shudder. Birmingham received most of the headlines, because it was that city which Dr. King selected as his target of the year. He put the children of Birmingham into the streets and Bull Connor, Birmingham's chief of police, arrested more than

Albany, Ga. convicted on federal charges of conspiracy and insurrection. Kennedy assassinated.

three thousand. In the late night hours of Mother's Day, the A. G. Gaston Motel where Dr. King was staying, and the home of Dr. King's brother, the Rev. A. D. King, were bombed. The response from Birmingham's black community was the first urban rebellion of the sixties. By the time the sun rose that Monday morning, some nine square blocks had been burned. Something new had been added to "the movement."

The South bent over backward to make it clear that it would rather fight than switch.

## THE WHITE MAN—II

"I have been
hanging people
for years, but I have
never
had all this fuss before."
Called to do the
honors
from the restaurant he owns,
Edward
("Lofty")
Milton, 54,
Rhodesia's part-time public
executioner
was professionally
incapable
of understanding the
commotion.

While African women clustered outside
Salisbury's Central Prison

and uttered the mournful wail of the Shona tribe,
"Wayche, wayche,"
Milton sprang the traps on the prison's
gallows
last week and sent
three
Rhodesian
blacks
spinning
into
eternity.

Then, returning to the
pleased
white patrons
of his Zambezi Valley cafe,
he sent off a
postcard
to a friend:

"Three
in
one
this time."

He signed it

"The
Dropper."

(*Time*—March 15, 1968)

White southerners have never engaged in intellectual
discussions concerning what happens within their
borders. Their response to any hints of social and
political change has been the gun and in 1963,
Jimmy Travis, a Mississippi SNCC worker, was shot
and almost killed outside of Greenwood one evening.
(It was the spring of 1966 when Jimmy, Worth
Long and I traveled together for a while. At least

once a day for several weeks, we drove past the spot where Jimmy had been shot. He would talk about it, the hours leading up to it, his misgivings about driving to Indianola that particular night, his thoughts and observations up to the instant he was shot. Since that night, though, he had been unable to bring himself to drive at night in Mississippi. One evening, as Worth got behind the wheel, Jimmy said, "Get in the back, muthafucka. I'm driving!" Worth looked at him. "It's about time, lazy nigger. I was getting ready to tell you that I wasn't your damn chauffeur." The last time I saw Jimmy was one foggy morning in May of that year. We were driving from Selma, Alabama, to Jackson, Mississippi, and Jimmy took the wheel. Bob Moses, who had been sitting beside Jimmy when he'd been shot, was in the back with some others. As we crossed the Mississippi line, someone said, "I can drive, man, if you getting tired." "I'm O.K.," Jimmy said. Through the fog Jimmy went, seventy, eighty miles an hour. I could see nothing through the window. The car lights shone on the fog without penetrating it, but Jimmy took every curve smoothly and evenly without slowing down. "I can see better at night," he said at one point. And he brought it on in. I had breakfast at his house and haven't seen him since. Last I heard he'd gotten married, joined the Muslims and was working in a foundry in Jackson.)

Jimmy Travis had been shot in the neck and miraculously lived. Medgar Evers died on his front porch, his wife and children standing in the door. The young blacks of Jackson were ready to go to war after the murder of Evers and on the day of the funeral it was only Attorney General Kennedy's emissary, John Doar, who prevented the war by stepping into that no man's land between the police and the young warriors. On the day of Evers' funeral, John Kennedy sent a civil rights bill to Congress. White people killed blacks with impunity and the Federal Government responded with a civil rights bill. The Kennedys reacted to black demands. They should've acted on the conditions and made the demands unnecessary. It was still the government of white people, by white people and for white people.

Nineteen sixty-three was the year the Mason-Dixon line disappeared. Blacks began demonstrating in the North and in New York City, blacks and whites sat-in at construction sites and more than seven hundred were arrested. In Philadelphia, more than fifty people were injured in demonstrations and of this number, half were policemen. There was a massive school boycott in Chicago. As more and more demonstrations took place against *de facto* segregation, whites were roused from their lethargic racism and began organizing for neighborhood schools. Small property owners organized against the black middle-class demands for open housing. There had never been a Mason-Dixon line. There were white people and there were niggers and wherever the twain met, all was well as long as the nigger was on the bottom and didn't try to get up. All had never been well and it was the illusion which was in the process of being destroyed.

The year came to a close when John Kennedy left Air Force One, feet first. If one is in public life, assassination holds out the possibility of being treated somewhat gently by history. Whatever John Kennedy was, he is now a minor saint because of the manner in which he died. In the lines which waited outside the Capitol while he lay in state, there were many blacks and reporters were anxious to interview them. White people needed to know that blacks still loved them and the more photographs which showed tears streaming down black faces, the more they were reassured. Massa Jack was gone and the darkies were in mourning. At least, that was what they wanted to believe.

The assassination of Kennedy caused America to lose a little faith in itself. It was therefore mandatory that the Warren Commission find Lee Harvey Oswald solely responsible for the deed. If one man had done it, it could be classified as an aberration of society. If there had been a conspiracy, the society itself would stand condemned and America could not condemn itself. It stood guilty of too much to allow the floodgates to be opened a fraction of an inch. But the doubts lingered and the fears of the fifties were added to by fears of unknown forces within the society that would murder the President. To murder the president of a country is to destroy that country's breathing symbol. America did not want to know what the assassination of Kennedy meant. Lee Harvey Oswald was the answer, but a minority was so convinced otherwise that they began their own investigations to prove that if Oswald were not innocent, he was at least not alone.

1964

February

School boy-

With the Republican Party's nomination of Barry Goldwater for the Presidency in 1964, the forces of

Armageddon gathered for battle. At least, that was the way it appeared then. The only thing which stood between the nation and utter destruction was Lyndon Baines Johnson. (Remember?) Many admitted that it was a contest between two evils, but, they rationalized, there was a qualitative difference between absolute evil and relative evil. They couldn't explain it, but they knew in their hearts they were right.

The young went to Mississippi that summer, to work in Freedom Schools, to help in voter registration campaigns, to do whatever needed to be done to help Mississippi blacks. Two of those who had come from the North were murdered. They came and their intentions were commendable, however misguided. (Was there any other course at that historical moment?) Eventually they would have to go back from whence they had come, but it was where the problem existed that they least wanted to be. They hated their community and their community hated them. So they came to Afroamerica, not realizing that they could never be citizens of that country. They could travel within its borders, but they would always remain outsiders. No one decreed that it should be that way.

December
800 arrested
on Berkeley
campus for
taking over
administra-
tion build-
ing.

That's simply how it was. That's how it would always be. They couldn't sing "I ain't gon' plow no cotton; ain't gon' hoe no corn." They were what they were—the children of affluence—and it was with each other that they would have to set up the next base camp in the search for the new land.

# 2.

(July 4, 1964
Washington, D.C.
1:30 A.M.

"Son, that bus goin' to Aiken, South Car'lina?"

"Where's the Memphis bus?"

"Now how they think all these folks gon' get on that bus?"

Black people going home. They have their usual traveling equipment—cardboard boxes tied with clothesline, suitcases held together with coarse rope, shopping bags, metal footlockers. Going South! The "block boys" and the old women, the young girls and their babies—going South! It's in the blood and years of living in the North can't exorcise it. The Negro was planted in the South and crop rotation won't keep the plant from returning to its first soil. No one but a Southerner, however, feels the pain that can be alleviated only by yearly pilgrimages.

No matter where he lives, no Southerner leaves the South.

July 5
Memphis, Tenn.
4 A.M.

The poor whites and the poor blacks. Only they ride the bus. Their accents may be different, but the same rope that binds their suitcases binds them to each other. There's one waiting room now and one people. The "crackers" and the niggers hang from the same cypress tree. Now that they are sitting in the same room, maybe they will realize it.

The Mississippi bus does not leave for three hours, but there is a rustle when the station announcer says, "Now leaving from Zone 7 for West Memphis, Hulbert, Edmondson, Round Pond, Widener, Madison, Forest City, Palestine, Wheatley, Fargo, Cotton Plant, Brinkley, Brasfield, Fredonia, De Valls Bluff and Little Rock. All aboard, please." What images in each mind do those names raise? If my father were here, Brinkley would mean a frame shack, getting up at dawn to work the cotton, cemeteries where his parents are buried and a place he left behind when he was seventeen. To me it means railroad tracks. That's all I remember from the once he took me there to see the house to which Dan Lester, his father, moved the family when they exchanged the Mississippi Delta for Arkansas.

I don't need to see if the bus just announced will be crowded. Those names mean too much for the bus to leave only half-filled. If you're from the South, home means more than your family and your friends. It means the heat of the interminable summer days; the trucks of field hands at dawn and the trucks returning at dusk; it's the dust beneath your feet on a back country road and it's the dust which drifts slowly across the fields and onto the porch when a car passes. It's the never big enough bottle of soda at the grocery store and it's sitting on the front porch at night, listening to the freight train switching boxcars. It's an announcer in a bus station saying, "All aboard, please, and thank you for traveling Greyhound."

July 5
Clarksdale, Miss.
10 A.M.

Hot already. Like Grandmother's kitchen on a summer day when she was heating irons in a tub of coals and cooking on the wood-burning stove at the same time. It is what one would expect, however, in the Mississippi Delta and in Clarksdale, "the blues capital of the world."

I've been traveling through the country that birthed Robert Johnson, Muddy Waters, Charlie Patton, Eli Green, Son House and Fred McDowell. It's flat, except for the trees protruding from the earth occasionally. All one sees is cotton—from the edge of the highway to the horizon—cotton. Sometimes a shack can be seen from the highway, but it merely looks like a different kind of cotton plant. Nothing takes your awareness away from the Delta. It is sky, land and heat—each one a plane that stretches interminably and relentlessly. Even the highway is the minimum, the essence of a highway. It is narrow and, unlike the super highways, Highway 61 does not impress itself on the surroundings.

Like the blues, the Delta is life in its essentialness. Sky and land. It is one line repeated twice and a rhyming last line—succinct and more than adequate in its expression.

Jackson, Miss.—July 5
Hattiesburg, Miss.—July 6
Hattiesburg, Miss.—July 7—late evening

Officially I came to Mississippi to sing in Freedom Schools, at mass meetings and to hold workshops on black music. Unofficially, though, I came to learn and to be born again. I came to see my family's beginning in this country. I want to go back to the beginning, to stand in the middle of a country road and feel what my slave great-grandparents felt. I want to see the landscape and the other slaves with their eyes. I want to hear them sing their songs, the songs I sing now. I want to be freed from slavery and feel the confusion and joy that emancipation brought. I want to stand in that road and hear field hollers and work songs change into the blues. I have a collective past, a past embracing the history of this country and the history of a people. My present was shaped by it. Right now, my past and my present are a sketch in chiaroscuro; I was a slave and now I am free. But chiaroscuro omits the gradations, the modulations from one key to another, the transition from slave to freedman. So, I am here. Mississippi. A pilgrimage to a cathedral of the Black Mass.

Gulfport, Miss.—July 9
Biloxi, Miss.—July 10—early afternoon

Has it only been five days since I boarded the bus at Port Authority in New York? Faith alone makes me believe that I have a wife and a "home" there. I do not know it. My knowledge has become limited to heat, to singing freedom songs, to sleeping in a different town each night and to being alone. My knowledge has increased to the degree that I am wary of any car that passes slowly down the street. The backfire of a truck or the loud slam of a screen door are identifiable as such only after I realize that no one has screamed. That, however, is no assurance that the next unnatural sound won't be followed by a scream. And possibly my own. I don't want to die, but no one does. Others, though, are willing to die for freedom. I'm not willing yet. Each morning I awake thinking, today I die.

Consciously or not, I think that many awake feeling the same. In some the fear is evident. In others it takes the form of a recklessness that verges on insanity at times. Sex, liquor and the speed of an automobile become the outlets for those who get no release in mass meetings. No one can live constantly with death without becoming mutilated or free.

The greatest courage, however, is living in Mississippi. Unfortunately, all you read and hear of are the harassments, the murders, beatings and jailings. The real stories, though, are of the Mississippi Negroes who walk to the courthouse to register to vote, knowing that loss of job or loss of life may be the consequence. The stories are of the Mississippi blacks who have opened their homes to white and black civil rights workers this summer and are not afraid to sit on their front porch in the evening and talk to the blond girl from Iowa while the traffic goes by. Courage is not dramatic; it is not an act easily observed by another, but courage is the norm in Mississippi.

Moss Point, Miss.—July 11
Jackson, Miss.—July 12—afternoon

Outside D'Lo, Mississippi, we saw an old black couple hitching a ride. It was a hot day, around noon. We stopped the car and they got in. They were going to town, to D'Lo for a bottle of pop. He was so drunk he could barely stand. She, at least, could do that, but not much more. We let them out in front of the grocery store and she borrowed a dime from me and as we drove away I wondered, how does "the movement" affect them? Will the civil rights bill have any effect in D'Lo, Mississippi? Or driving back from Moss Point, we saw a young couple sitting beside a car. We stopped. They'd had a flat and didn't have a spare. The girl was cute in her dirty, torn yellow party dress. Her hand was bleeding and she was holding it in a piece of dirty brown paper. "Where're you from?" we asked. "Chicago," she smiled. Then she laughed. "Collins, Mississippi." She bummed a cigarette and asked if we were "freedom riders." All civil rights workers in Mississippi are called "freedom riders," whether they were actually on the Freedom Rides or not. As we drove off they resumed their seats by the side of the road, having refused our proffered aid. Who knows? Maybe they're sitting there now, unperturbed by it all, waiting for Godot. Or there're the houses by the road or the two little boys I saw walking on the wrong side of the road at dusk, or the truck filled with white kids who made faces and yelled as we passed them. It makes you wonder,

wonder when fear and terror will not be the atmos-
phere in which one walks and talks, eats and sleeps.
All of this hurts me because I am impotent. There
is nothing I can do to relieve the injustices, the
miseries. Say a kind word, register a voter, sing a
song, but there'll always be D'Lo, Mississippi. Simultaneously there will be love and laughter, sex and
children, dancing and playing, the beauties of mountains and rivers, Bach and Scarlatti, Rembrandt and
Malcolm Lowry, and somehow I'm still unable to
reconcile the joy and the sorrow. Yes, they are one,
a part of a bigger whole; each is necessary and
should not be thought of as just or unjust, beautiful
or ugly. Nonetheless it angers me that beauty has
to have ugliness walk beside it, that all that exists
does exist and no one person can alleviate all of it.
None of us will ever be free until we love, really
love, and understand and sacrifice and be willing
to lay down our lives for our brothers, until we
aren't clogged up with our own desires and interests,
until we aren't concerned with making people like us,
but with knowing another like we know ourselves, to
cry when another cries, whether he be in the same
room or a million miles away. I can't say those
things, because they seem so alien to everyone, so
foreign and so irrelevant. Maybe they are.

Tougaloo, Miss.—July 13
early A.M.

Today was a vacation. I needed it. After sleeping
most of the day I went over to Hellen's house. I guess
it's a mistake for two sad people to spend a day
together. Particularly a mouse-gray, rainy day on a
lonely road.

"Sometimes I'm sad for months and all I do is
drink. I'm either sad or happy, you know. Never in-
between. It has to be that way. If you're an intense
person, that's the only way it can be."

Hellen is twenty-three and she's from Clarksdale.
She's short, medium brown-skinned, with eyes that
can't be lied to. In two days she is leaving for Mc-
Comb, Mississippi, one of the most dangerous cities
in the state.

"One time I went down in that area with Casey
and Mary. We just wanted to get away for a day,
so we went down there looking for the Natchez
Trace. We didn't find it, but we came upon this ghost
house. These two tall white columns standing back
of a grove of trees. They were just standing there.
It was strange. You know? There they were in the
midst of all this silence."

Hellen has been in "the movement" since she
finished high school. For her it was the natural thing
to do.

"I like you because you know a lot of sad songs.
I wish I could play the guitar. Could you teach me
to play 'Another Man Done Gone'? That's my favor-
ite song. Somebody taught me to play it once, but
I never had a guitar to practice on."

It was raining now and night had emerged from
the all day grayness. We were both drinking bourbon as I showed her how to finger an E minor chord.
It didn't matter that she wouldn't learn to play it
that night. It didn't matter that she had a difficult
time carrying a tune when I wasn't singing with her.
I don't know if I can say what did matter. Maybe
the bourbon. It could do something we couldn't. It
could obliterate the thought of half of a man's body

draped over a log in the river. It could make me not care about the four thousand lynchings and more that have occurred in America. It could make me forget how long and empty a Mississippi highway is at night, how few houses there are and how many miles and miles of forests there are with dirt roads disappearing into them.

She was only twenty-three and for three years she had done what should have been unnecessary. How much hate can one individual feel directed at him before his soul fills with a sadness that penetrates even his happy moments?

She is an old woman and I am an old man and the same trees from which so many blacks were hanged are being washed by the rain tonight. The rain beats on the roofs of the lynched and the lynchers. It soaks into the charred wood of a bombed church and runs down the stained-glass windows of another.

The grass is green on the banks of the rivers, but when you go fishing, take along a winding sheet.

It is late now and I must sleep. There isn't much any one man can do in this life, but each man should do what he has to and when he has to. Sometimes it is nothing more than making a pilgrimage. Another time it will be nothing more than dying.

If it must be, so be it.)

# 3.

1965

**January**

4 blacks arrested in N.Y.C. for allegedly plotting to blow up the Statue of Liberty.

**February**

U.S. bombs North Vietnam.

**March**

Selma-Montgomery March. One killed. SDS demonstrates against Chase Manhattan Bank for its South Africa investments. Vietnam teach-in at Univ. of Michigan attracts 3,000. 25,000 march

The encounters with Afroamerica brought a simultaneous retreat from a world that was too much with us and we were too much with ourselves, not knowing how to reach out to touch the hand of another and not be ashamed. No one knew himself, or why he did what he did, or what he was doing when he was doing it. He did it, cashed the check every Friday and did it again the next week and never knew why. If we had been a nation of farmers, a back-to-the-land movement would've started, but being a nation whose only roots are in rootlessness, whose only tradition is motion, the retreat was to time before, when we were young and it was fun to be a child. Giant posters of Superman and The Phantom and other comic book heroes of the past were printed and sold in great quantity. Back, back "to those thrilling days of yesteryear. The Lone Ranger rides again!" Back, back to the days when Jack Armstrong (The Aaaaaaall American Boy!) was on

on Washington to protest war. 12,000 attend teach-in at Berkeley.

U.S. invades Dominican Republic.

**Summer**

SNCC organizes all-black political party in Alabama. Students in Berkeley try to stop troop train. Draft card burnings begin.

**August**

WATTS

**October**

100,000 across country protest war.

**November**

Norman Morrison, Roger La-Porte and Alice Hertz immolate themselves to protest war.

the radio at 5:30 as mother set the table and Vietnam was not a suburb of Dubuque, Iowa.

The young had never known such a world. When supper was defrosted and heated in their house, Huntley and Brinkley were summarizing the machinations of yet another day's petty pace. "In Vietnam today, U.S. Marines fought their way out of a Vietcong ambush, leaving 1,047 Vietcong dead and one Marine bleeding from scratching his mosquito bites too hard." In their search, they crowded the art theaters to watch the more than ever popular films of W. C. Fields, The Marx Brothers, and Humphrey Bogart. ("Play it again, Sam," Bogie said. Sam was the nigger in the flick and I kept telling him, "Don't play it again, Sam. If that white man wants to hear the damn song so much, let him learn to play the piano his own damn self and you go get a little taste of Ingrid Bergman's pussy." But Sam played it again.) Bogie was a man. There was nothing complex in his world; good was good and evil was evil and Bogie crushed it, despite himself. He wasn't the traditional knight in shining armor. The young generation knew that no one was good. Bogie disguised

December
40,000 pro-
test war in
Washington.
his goodness and his sentimentality in a rough exterior—the craggy face, the brusque voice, the cigarette dangling from the corner of the mouth. He wasn't about to be taken in by anybody or anything. He wasn't about to let anybody get away with anything he thought was wrong, either.

The young generation agreed. They protested the inhumanity of a death-centered country and by saying NO, regained a portion of their own humanity and came alive. They sang "I Ain't A-Marching Anymore" with Phil Ochs and with Dylan they knew that the answer was blowing in the wind. They slowly left the old people with the old songs for new protest songs which they wrote and sang. It was themselves and their world they were reflecting and there was much to protest—the war in Vietnam, segregation, slums, violence, Lyndon Johnson. But they could think of few solutions except love. They had never been loved and it was this searching for love which framed all of their activities. MAKE LOVE NOT WAR, they said and Peter, Paul and Mary sang "Because All Men Are Brothers Wherever They May Be" (but no one is quite sure where They Be) while brothers in the South ducked Klansmen bullets and brothers in Vietnam ducked U.S. Army bullets. Pete Seeger sang about his hammer of justice, freedom and love and about hammering out these things all over this land while others hammered out fractured skulls and limbs on the backroads of Mississippi and the back alleys of Chicago.

Love. Yes, people *should* love each other. Yes,

everyone *should* live in peace and harmony and everybody *should* have enough to eat and nobody *should* be without anything he needs and black people *should* have freedom and on and on the list could go of what *should* be but isn't because the world is composed of what is. It's simply a matter of who has the power to enforce what he thinks should be.

# three

# 1.

At first, few cared about Vietnam. Few even knew.
A small number of American soldiers were there as
"advisers," and "advising" was a role America
thought itself especially suited for. Americans had
advised the less privileged of the world on such mat-
ters as religion, trade, economy, business and culture
for almost half a century. Whatever "advice" the
Army was giving the Vietnamese, there was no
doubt that it was for their own good. (Joan and I
were still on that first plateau of love where one does
not have enough hands with which to know the other,
where there are not enough minutes to do the know-

ing, where one tries to become sated with the other and is continually frustrated because it is not possible, when one Saturday afternoon in the fall of 1962, one of those autumn afternoons that is all the more delicious because it will soon give way to winter gray, we found ourselves walking along Seventh Avenue near Times Square. On the triangular island dividing Seventh Avenue and Broadway where the Armed Forces Recruiting Station sits, a small group of kids were marching with picket signs. GET OUT OF VIETNAM. NO MORE DIEN BIEN PHU! I wanted to ask Joan who was Dien Bien Phu, but I assumed it must've been the name of some South Vietnamese dictator. We watched the pickets for a few minutes and then went our way through our pale yellow world on our Saturday afternoon.)

Slowly, more and more "advisers" were being sent to South Vietnam and the press began to hint that they were doing more than "advising." Then, one day, in some month, without anyone announcing that we were at war, everyone knew.

It was Lyndon Johnson's fate to have to justify the war to which Kennedy had committed seventeen thousand men and being from another place and another time, Johnson's arguments had no relationship to the reality of the sixties: "When they lead your boy down to that railroad station to send him into boot camp and put a khaki uniform on him to send him some place where he may never return, they don't ask you whether you are a Republican or a Democrat. They send you there to defend that flag, and you go." Johnson was from that time when the President needed only to ask for the country's support and it was his. (Or at least that's what they want us to believe.) Johnson could remember when it was the noblest of sentiments to love one's country, to fight willingly, and if necessary, die for the Stars and Stripes. But those who had grown up in the shadow of Hiroshima ("Mama, can I play in the rain?" "No, dear. I think you'd better stay inside and play. The rain is radioactive.") wondered if there weren't higher priorities than defending the flag. Indeed, it could be asked if defending the flag were a priority at all.

By the spring of 1965, the young had begun to organize against the war. They were joined by many intellectuals (who may have used the war as a weapon to show their contempt for a President who came from a different class than they). They worked with the students and organized "teach-ins," where students came and stayed all night, listening to discussions on the history of Vietnam, the Geneva Convention, American foreign policy, the economics and politics of Southeast Asia.

It was natural that the young should be concerned about the war, for it was the young who were being asked to fight. The reasons for this particular war were even more obscure than the reasons given for the Korean war. Not only was there no clear-cut right and wrong, some began to feel that if there were, the United States might be on the side of wrong. Others did not go so far as to try and ascertain who was right and who was wrong. For them it was enough that a war was being fought and people were dying. They refused to be a part of it under any circumstances and if the consequences were jail, they were willing to be imprisoned. They would not kill another human being.

## THE WAR—I

Marines at Khe Sanh
sometimes
see bodies flung into the air
by the
explosions
when
the bombs are dumped
directly
on the
enemy
trenches.

As Major Billy F. Munley,
an observation pilot
who directs the
bombing
of
targets
around Khe Sanh,
describes the scene:

"It
looks
like
the world
caught
smallpox
and
died."

(*Time*—April 5, 1968)

It was a war no one understood, few really
wanted, but most defended. A guerrilla war, it was
called. The enemy was everywhere and nowhere.
An American didn't know if the Vietnamese serving

him lunch would be shooting at him a few hours later. The child to whom you just gave candy, the prostitute you screwed the night before, the people riding by on bicycles—anyone could be a V.C. The frontline was the Vietnamese closest to you, even if it were an old man napping in the shade. (Especially if it were an old man napping in the shade.)

Whether or not America should've become involved became a moot question. We were there and honor dictated that we had to win. It was unthinkable to let a bunch of rice-eaters defeat the greatest military power the world had ever seen. If America could not win the war, there were other rice-eaters in Asia, who might decide that they, too, could try the same thing. And there were spear-throwers in Africa and sombrero-wearers in Latin America who would be fighting for the right to be their own "advisers." In fact, if the United States didn't win in Vietnam, it would lose everywhere.

The State Department told us that it was a war of Communist aggression. The Vietnamese said it was a war of national liberation. The State Department said there were no such things as "wars of national liberation." The young didn't believe it. All they could see was the United States in someone else's country. It had no right to be there. If it didn't leave, then it should be defeated and more and more began rooting for "the enemy." Some even carried the flag of the National Liberation Front on demonstrations. VICTORY FOR THE NLF!

To those who had grown up in ancient times, such sentiments were worse than treason. They agreed with President Johnson: "Let's just see if we can't find something good about America, and let's see if we can't take pride in that flag, and let's see if we can't have a little feeling well up in us and see if we can't get down on our knees sometimes during the night and thank God that I am an American.

"I have traveled around the world and I have been in many countries, and I have even seen the glories of art and architecture. I have seen the sun rise on Mont Blanc. But the most beautiful vision that these eyes ever beheld was that American flag in a foreign land."

What to Lyndon Johnson was "the most beautiful vision" was the most repulsive to the young. To them the American flag was synonymous with everything that was wrong with the world. America was the enemy of humanity and the Vietcong the benefactors. It was they who were the heroes, they, Fidel, Che, the Cuban people and the good Chairman. ("Whom would you rather sleep with? Ho Chi Minh or House Speaker McCormick?" The girl couldn't answer for laughing so hard. "Whom would you rather sleep with?" she tittered, gasping for breath. "Fidel or Lyndon?" The game went around the country for a while and the results showed that America's young women would rather fuck revolutionaries.) The war clarified a lot for the young. They had rejected their parents (fleshly manifestations of America), but blackness, their first alternative, was only partially open to them. The war gave them an identity. They wanted to be revolutionaries.

### THE ENEMY

In the quiet hours
just before dawn,
Viet Cong gunners

by twos and threes
slipped from hiding places
on the outskirts of Saigon
and hurriedly set up the simple launching tubes
of their 122-mm. rockets.

Without bothering to take careful aim,
they pointed the tubes in the direction of the
sleepy capital city.
Then,
one after another,
there were brief flashes of backblast
and the keening sound 41-pound warheads
whistling off into the
morning sky.

Moments later,
the deadly missiles slammed into Saigon,
exploding in streets and squares,
homes and shops,
rousing their unlucky victims
with a final,
emphatic reveille.

And long before the dust from the blasts settled,
the Communist gun crews
had disappeared without a trace
into the surrounding swamplands.

(*Newsweek*—June 24, 1968)

The young went into the streets to demonstrate
their commitment to the people of South Vietnam.
Many burned their draft cards publicly. Some
stabbed America in the heart and burned American
flags. Thousands refused to go into the army when
the old men ordered them. Thousands more decided
to become teachers, which, in many areas, is a draft-

exempt occupation. Joan Baez stood up at an antiwar rally in New York and told girls only to say
yes to boys who said no. And who knows how many
hundreds of thousands found honor and manhood
and glory in being a faggot on the day they went
to report for their physical.

## 2.

### SOLDIER—I

This is my Rifle.
There are many like it,
but this one is
my friend.
I must master it
as I master my life.

My rifle
without me,
is useless.
I must fire my rifle true.
I must shoot straighter than
my enemy
who is trying
to kill me.
I must shoot him
before he shoots me.
I will.

My rifle and myself know
that what counts in this war

is not the rounds we fire,
the noise of our burst,
nor the smoke we make.
We know that
it is the
hits that count.
We will hit.

My rifle is human,
even as I,
because it is my life.
Thus,
I will learn it as a brother.
We will become part of each other.

Before God
I swear this creed.
My rifle and myself
are the defenders of my country.
We are the masters
of our enemy.
We are the saviours
of my life.

So be it,
until victory is America's
and there is no enemy,
but peace!

(The Parris Island Marine Yearbook)

Some went when they received their notices. Not that they particularly wanted to or because they were patriotic. The prospect of five years in jail appeared to be a worse alternative than the Army. So they went, followed orders, and if they were lucky, came back home alive.

### SOLDIER—II

At 7:45,
three more marines
were carried in.
One was a Negro,
wide awake on a stretcher,
calmly answering questions.
He didn't realize that
his left leg
had been torn off
just below the knee—
or that his right foot
was hanging
only by tendons and flesh.
A doctor nodded to a corpsman
standing at the foot of the stretcher.
Quickly,
the corpsman picked up
a pair of surgical scissors
and started to cut the
mangled foot away from the ankle.
"My leg, my leg,"
screamed the marine.
The amputation
was finished in seconds
and another corpsman
carried
away the bone and flesh
still packed inside
the bloody combat boot.
The marine,
shot full of morphine,
was soon quiet.

(*Newsweek*—March 25, 1968)

There were those so young that for the brief

amount of time they lived, they might as well have never been born.

## SOLDIER—III

Charlie Mack Gilmer was just 19
"the best-looking boy in Plum Creek."
He dropped out of high school,
but he used to tell his little brother Herbert
he'd break his neck if he didn't pass the fifth grade.
Last November, Mack was drafted.
On May 23, while he was on sentry duty
in a village close to Chu Lai
a sniper picked him off.
When his body was brought back,
"You couldn't get into the funeral,"
says his widowed mother.
"Mack took care of us," Mrs. Gilmer sighs
(there are ten other children).
"He didn't know much about the war.
But he went like a man."

(*Newsweek*—August 10, 1967)

Death is absurd. A ridiculous thing, lying in a coffin, eyes closed, and you look at the body and it's the person, yet, something is missing. You can lift the veil from the coffin, touch the skin, kiss the cheek, but you don't understand what it is that's missing. It's more than breath being taken in and expelled by the lungs. It's more than the beating of the heart. Something else is missing and you don't know what it is, so you say, "He's gone." "He's dead." "He passed away." That does not explain the absence of a voice which was there a few days ago. That does not explain the sweaters on a

hanger in the closet, waiting to be filled. To say
that someone is dead explains nothing. It simply
states an unfathomable fact.

### THE WAR—II

Mrs. John Smith of Nashville, Tenn.,
the wife of a cameraman
for the Columbia Broadcasting System,
has been living in the Caravelle
for nearly a year.

From her terrace
she watched
tanks and troops
move beneath her,
watched the barbed wire
drawn into a net
around the National Assembly Building
across the street,
watched
two truckloads
of dead Americans
being driven by.

"It was the
first time
I've ever seen
so many
dead people
at once,"

she said.

(*The New York Times*—February 3, 1968)

Most absurd is life continuing in the midst of death.
Life hardly pauses to acknowledge the dying, unless it is a John or Robert Kennedy, or a Martin

Luther King. But who are they that the world should be more mindful of their deaths than of Charles Mack Gilmer's? But if death is absurd, maybe life is even more so.

### THE WAR—III

And from the outskirts of the city
the napalm
could be seen
spewing up
in a giant burst
of
smoke and flame.
It makes an odd picture.
Between
the
city
and the
napalm explosions,
farmers work their rice paddies.

(*The New York Times*—March 23, 1968)

(Easter Sunday, 1967
Thanh Hoa Province, North Vietnam

It was shortly after noon when the bombing started. I was lying down when suddenly I heard a loud WOOM! in the distance. It sounded like thunder, but it was a sunny, clear day. I leaped out of bed and ran outside. WOOM! WOOM! On the horizon I could see a trail of black smoke. I and the other Americans were the only ones paying it any attention. Nearby, a Vietnamese woman and her little girl were weeding. They did not show the slightest sign that they had heard anything. And, perhaps they hadn't. For over a year, the planes had been coming everyday. Now it was normal.

Later in the afternoon, the planes came closer and I saw three jets swoop low over a clump of trees. In the fields, the peasants continued plowing, without looking skyward. They knew by the sound that the planes were not close enough to attack them. I wasn't sure. I could imagine those "crackers" eating breakfast this morning, going to church services and hearing all about the risen Christ, drinking communion and then running and jumping into the cockpits of their planes and roaring off to celebrate Easter.

Later that afternoon I was sitting in the outhouse when a plane came quite close. For a moment I thought it would be just my fate to get killed in the middle of a good shit. But I relaxed, figuring that the secret village where we were staying was well enough camouflaged that I could finish relieving myself. I was right, but what had begun as a pleasure, ended as a duty.

At dusk, the bombing ended.)

### THE WAR—IV

The first obstacle
the colonel encountered
was not bursting shells
or
weeping refugees.
It was a wedding party
threading its way
past the armored personnel carriers,
machine guns
and soldiers

whose belts
sagged
under the weight of hand grenades.

The bride was radiant.
The groom was silent.
The wedding guests,
clad in black and white robes,
smiled. In the distance,
in a thicket of green palms,
there was the sound
of an explosion.

The colonel tightened his grip on his rifle.
The wedding party marched along.
A few yards away,
past a row of sagging houses with rusting tin roofs,
women were washing clothes
and rinsing rice
in a sluggish yellow creek.

(*The New York Times*—January 26, 1968)

The dying die. The living live.

### THE WAR—V

On the tenth floor terrace
of the Hotel Caravelle,
foreigners
and well-to-do refugees
calmly sipped their gin and tonics
as television cameras
recorded the scene below.
And in a comfortable villa
barely 200 yards from the spot where
General Loan was wounded,
a young British couple

gossiped cosily over drinks. "I think
he's a *terrible* man,"
said the girl. "Whenever he comes
into the office,
I simply curl up."
A recoilless rifle barked nearby.
"Does he irritate you, too?
Oh, good, I'm so glad."

(*Newsweek*—May 20, 1968)

And when death becomes entertainment at dinner,
it tells us what life has become.


### THE WAR—VI

At the restaurant atop the Caravelle Hotel,
customers clamored for window seats
and then sat
eating steak and lobster
and
watching planes and helicopters
strafing the city's outskirts.

Nearby,
at the United States officers club atop the Rex Hotel,
captains and majors
munched hamburgers
and
leaned out the windows
to catch a glimpse
of the fighting.

When the thump of rockets
drifted
up
to
the
club,

one man tore himself away from
a row of
slot machines
to look out over the city.

After satisfying himself
that the building
was in no immediate danger,
he returned
to the slot machines.

On the streets below,
vendors did a brisk business in
black-market cigarettes at
50 cents a pack.

"Dirty pictures—American girls,"
one vendor called out
in an effort to bring customers to his stall.

(*The New York Times*—May 8, 1968)

Wars have always been fought for land and the
victory came when one adversary conquered that of
the other. The Vietnam war was different. Victories
were not found in capturing the Porkchop Hills and
the Iwo Jimas. Victory came in the "body-count."
Drop those bombs! Fire those mortars! Kill! Kill!
Kill! Whoever outkilled the other was the winner.
It was simple and all it called for was people trained
to do the killing. But in Vietnam, the United States
was faced with an enemy whose first line of defense
was the minds of the people. If the people understood why they were fighting, if they understood
whom they were fighting, and if they understood
for what they were fighting, they would have the
will to fight for a hundred years. The Vietnamese

have been defeating one enemy after another for more than a quarter of a century.

The United States realized slowly that if it were going to win the war, it had to fight that battle for the minds of the people. Soldiers were instructed in Vietnamese customs and told to respect the local people, to try and make friends with them.

### WINNING FRIENDS—I

"While the people
are going through the wreckage
of their homes
trying to save something,"
growls a student,
"the American troops
sit there
in the sun,
eating their lunch,
joking
and
listening to the radio.
The two things should not be
that close."
And indeed,
the two groups
somehow
seem to be inhabiting
different worlds;
late last week,
as a group of somber
Vietnamese poked through a
heap of blackened metal in District Eight,
a frolicking
GI leaped into their midst
in pursuit of

an errant
baseball.

(*Newsweek*—May 27, 1968)

The United States tried to win friends in Vietnam as it had tried to raise its young; by promising her freedom but giving her Arpège.

## WINNING FRIENDS—II

The United States Army
said today
that members of the
Fourth Psychological Operations Group
would soon begin handing out
small packages of
cigarettes,
each imprinted with a
propaganda message.

The 100,000 packages will be
distributed to
prisoners and detainees
during interrogation periods.
Teams will later pass out
the cigarettes
to Vietnamese
in
hamlets and villages.

Each package,
containing four cigarettes,
is imprinted with the Vietnamese-language abbreviations
for
the Republic of Vietnam.
The package wrappings are
red

and
yellow,
the colors of the South Vietnamese
flag.
The packages will be inscribed:
"The Government of Vietnam
cares for
its people."

(*The New York Times*—April 14, 1968)

The war won no friends, in Vietnam or at home. The war did not cause the heart to pound from the halls of Montezuma to the shores of Tripoli. Those who returned from the war were not welcomed by marching bands. They were hardly welcomed at all. From time to time there would be a White House ceremony and the President would pin medals on some guy who had fought more fiercely to save his life than most, but few looked upon these medal-winners as heroes. To the young they were fools for having gone and lucky to have made it back. Once it had been an honor to wear the uniform of the United States Armed Services. No longer, and the soldiers knew it.

### SOLDIER—IV

At night,
the men in Corporal Noyes's bunker
sit
and
talk,
sing
or
play cards.

During a night when more than 1,000 rounds
hit Khesanh,
Corporal Noyes turned to a friend
and said:

"Man, it'll be really decent
to go home
and never hear words like
incoming shells,
mortars,
rifles
and all that stuff.
And the first guy
who asks me how it feels
to kill
I'll . . ."

A pause,
then he said:
"You know,
my brother wants me to go duck hunting
when I get home.
Man, I don't want to
even see a slingshot
when I get out of here."

Still later, he called out:
"Okay, we're going to sing now.
Anyone who can't sing has to hum.
Because I said so.
O.K. let's hear it."
Lance Cpl. Richard Morris,
24,
of North Hollywood, Calif.,
began playing a guitar.
Two favorites that night were
"500 Miles,"
and "Where Have All The Flowers Gone?"

A hard emphasis accompanied the part that went:
"Where have all the soldiers gone?
To the graveyard everyone.
Oh, when will they ever learn?
Oh, when will they ever learn?"

Finally,
the two small bulbs
were turned out
and
the marines
struggled toward sleep.

(*The New York Times*—February 13, 1968)

They had been drafted. They went. They took orders, counted the days until they could go home, and, they prayed. They had been told many times why they were fighting, but if a man doesn't know why he's fighting, no amount of telling him will matter. They were fighting to stay alive and get back home, regardless of what the Pentagon said.

### SOLDIER—V

Lynda Bird's husband,
Marine Capt. Charles Robb,
hasn't been
idling
these weeks
before he leaves for
Vietnam.
He spends
time studying
Vietnamese practical phrases
in case
of any
emergencies.

One of the
first
phrases
he learned
is
how to say
"I am hurt."

(*New York Post*—March 28, 1968)

On the battlefields of Vietnam, the only passion came with the agonized crying of wounded men in the fear of death. On the battlefields of America, the passion came with shouts of HELL, NO! WE WON'T GO! The government said we must support our boys in Vietnam. The protesters agreed; BRING THEM HOME!

(It was a bright, sun-warmed October Saturday in Washington, D.C. Good demonstration weather. I had come to Washington the previous afternoon on the train and spent the night at Ivanhoe's, talking until near dawn about Africa, SNCC, Stokely and each other, what we were thinking and doing and why. I was up and in the streets soon after first light, because I wanted to get a feel of the city on the day of what was to be the largest antiwar demonstration of the sixties, if not in American history.

At the White House, extra guards were on duty and White House tours had been cancelled for the day. I stood at the fence on the Pennsylvania Avenue side for a few minutes, looking through the bars, across the green lawn at the big white building where so many decisions were made that affected my life. It was about nine, but already the "long-haired" ones could be seen strolling amiably down the street. Some had packs on their backs and sleeping bags over their shoulders. They looked harmless and so young with their shoulder-length hair.

The morning went slowly and I meandered over to the Washington Monument and watched them coming in small groups from every direction. All morning they came. How clean and good and untouched by life they seemed, filled with good will and indignation.

It was practically an all-white crowd. The few blacks there had come, like myself, to see some white folks get their asses kicked, because this was to be the day.

It was midafternoon before the actual march on the Pentagon began. The morning had been consumed with the inevitable speeches which said what everybody already knew and no one could hear, but people who hadn't seen each other since the last big demonstration had a chance to get reacquainted and new people had a chance to meet other new people and radical groups sold buttons and newspapers and posters and books and bumper stickers and pamphlets all calling for the revolution and telling how to do it and where to do it and who to quote. I wandered through the crowds like the alien I was, taking pictures of girls lying with their heads in guy's laps, of old women with the kind of beauty that comes only with having felt a lot and seen a lot and done a lot and knowing that there was still a lot to do, of proud young girls in miniskirts and beads and long earrings and sandals in the beauty of earnest youth, of cops and cops and cops and of

a young black kid, beads around his neck, who came
up to me as I sat on the steps of the Lincoln Memorial and gently offered me a stick of marijuana
which I refused, but felt good because he was so
young and so beautiful and I prayed that he could
keep that beauty and not have it dynamited when
it was his turn to buy the groceries, pay the rent
and the phone bill, get the laundry done, the clothes
cleaned, the prescriptions filled and all the rest that
comes when it's you and not momma and daddy
who has to be the adult, the grown-up.

Eventually, the march began, filling the bridge
across the Potomac, the Lincoln Memorial behind,
the graves of Robert E. Lee and John F. Kennedy
in front. (Birds of a feather get buried together.)
Across a field the march went and under a bridge
on which stood Virginia state troopers who looked
like Mississippi Alabama Georgia state troopers,
their hands resting lightly on the butts of their
guns, two of them leaning easily on the WELCOME
TO VIRGINIA sign, but no one charged up the
hill like the troopers were hoping and wishing and
praying.

The march wound its way onto one of the parking
lots of the Pentagon and there, standing above the
trees, were the corpse gray walls of the Pentagon
itself. That was where Robert McNamara went to
work everyday and made the decisions and ordered
the weapons and looked at the maps and received
the reports and counted the deaths.

The march was to have ended at the parking lot,
where more speeches were to have been given and
for those who wanted to protest, it had been ar-

ranged with the Government that there would be a symbolic line across which they would step and be arrested, but when the people got there and saw that building, that building, they forgot about symbolic protests and immediately started running toward the Pentagon. Before the troops and marshals had realized it, the fence separating the parking lot from the Pentagon Mall had been torn down and the demonstrators were toe-to-toe with the troops in the driveway leading to the Pentagon.

The sun was still shining as the people, arm in arm and hand in hand, filled the Pentagon mall, filled the driveway up which McNamara's limousine had come that very morning. For a while, nothing happened. The young looked at the troops and Federal marshals, who stood in the driveway between them and the building itself. For several hours it was like that until the young massed in the driveway suddenly broke through the line of troops and with a loud cheer, ran up the driveway for the door of the Pentagon. Up the oval driveway they went running running running, heads down, hair blowing in the wind, knowing that they were going to be clubbed once they got to that doorway but they were so young and oh so beautiful and didn't seem to care or maybe they just didn't have any better sense which is one of the great things about being young. After that there were continual breaks through the lines. The soldiers, most of them not much older than the "long-haired ones," tried to keep the crowds under control, but how do you control people who laugh when you point your rifle at them? How do you control people who stick long-stemmed flowers

in the barrel of your rifle? You don't. You can sub-
due them, but they will never be controlled.

Eventually, night came and with it, the cold and
the dew. Most of the demonstrators left, but those
remaining removed their sleeping bags from their
shoulders, spread them on the grass and settled
down for the evening.)

### THE MAKING OF REVOLUTIONARIES

As the minutes to midnight
ticked away,
the protesters—
some bearded
and almost all
dressed or wrapped in an
odd
assortment of
shirts,
slacks,
jackets,
blankets,
and sleeping bags—
burst into song.
First,
they sang the old
civil rights standby,
"We Shall Overcome."
Then,
they swung into
"America the Beautiful."

The phrase—
"and crown thy good with brotherhood"—
was hanging in the air
as the Federal officials

moved in
and seized the first of the
protesters,
a girl
clad in a bright orange shirt.

(*The New York Times*—October 23, 1967)

# four

# 1.

1966
January
4 H-bombs
fall from
U.S. bomber
off the coast
of Spain.
Black college
student,
Sammy Younge,
Jr., murdered
in Alabama.
SNCC issues
statement
against the

America was in the midst of a revolution, but the guerrillas were not coming down from the hills. They were walking out the front doors of their homes, crossing the lawn and disappearing into San Francisco's Haight-Ashbury, New York's East Village and various other liberated zones. They were as young as fourteen, but they left, by the thousands. They were not runaways but deserters, going AWOL from the American way of life. Where the Beat Genera-

war in Vietnam. Georgia legislature refuses to seat Julian Bond.

February

Kwame Nkrumah deposed as head of Ghana.

March

Sukarno deposed in Indonesia.

June

James Meredith shot in Miss. Richard Speck kills 8 nurses in Chicago. Stokely Carmichael articulates concept of Black Power. Black Rebellions.

July

Black Rebellions.

August

Luci Baines Johnson marries.

tion had been a small, isolated phenomenon of men and women in their twenties and thirties, the Cultural Revolution of the mid-sixties was a mass assault by children on every value America considered decent.

Marijuana, once a drug used by jazz musicians and blacks, became the letter A in the dictionary of the new self-definition. It was smoked as casually and as openly as a dog pissing on the street. LSD went beyond "grass" with its strange power to transform the mind's way of apprehending the world. One saw, felt, and listened differently. Another world was created and some returned from that world with a vision of what they could be. Others liked the other world so much that they began living just for the excursions into that world.

The young women shed their clothes as if they were a part of that self which they wanted to kill. No longer were their legs impeded by the hems of skirts and dresses as they walked down the street. Hemlines stopped a few inches below the hips. Some men considered the miniskirt an acknowledgment of accessibility, but the short skirts were merely recognition of the fact that

King leads
demonstra-
tions in Chi-
cago.
Black re-
bellions.
Joseph Whit-
man shoots
44 people,
killing 14,
from a tower
in Texas.
September
Verwoerd,
head of
U.S.A.,
assassinated.
Whites beat
black school
children in
Grenada,
Miss.

the legs of a woman are a sensual delight apart from the touching of them.

With the coming of the miniskirt, the era of the breast ended and fashion models had to be slim, with only a hint of breast, enough to establish the fact that they were female, but little more. The hair was cut short, cropped to fit the head. Twiggy was the ultimate, a little boy in women's clothes and the triumph of the homosexual male in the fashion industry was complete. He had his revenge on women.

All that was sacred to parents (America) was a target of guerrilla warfare for the young. Virginity, once prized like a brick of Fort Knox gold, was now an historical artifact to be laughed at. The cars which fathers meticulously washed and waxed in the driveways (with strips of grass down the middle) were painted every fantastic color under the sun with stickers on the rear fender that didn't say WE SAW CARLSBAD CAVERNS. Inside the cars they sat, their garments festooned with buttons, each a well-aimed bullet to the hearts of their parents.

HELP STAMP OUT UGLINESS! STERILIZE LBJ!
WHERE IS LEE HARVEY OSWALD NOW THAT WE
    NEED HIM?

NO EASTER—THEY FOUND THE BODY!
GOD IS NOT DEAD. HE JUST DOESN'T WANT TO
  GET INVOLVED.
GOD IS NOT DEAD. HE JUST MOVED TO A BETTER
  NEIGHBORHOOD.
WAR IS GOOD BUSINESS. INVEST YOUR SON.
OLD SOLDIERS NEVER DIE. YOUNG ONES DO.
GOD HAS SIMPLY GONE UNDERGROUND.
MAIM A CHILD FOR DEMOCRACY.
GET BEHIND LBJ—HELP ME PUSH.
THE MEEK SHALL INHERIT THE EARTH. THEY
  CAN HAVE IT.
GO NAKED.
PLAN AHEAD. USE CONTRACEPTIVES.

They were casual, if not cynical, about those things which their parents took seriously and serious about that which their parents thought little of. Your friends were the people you liked to be with, the young insisted, not those who could best help you "get ahead." Living was something you did everyday, not two weeks once every fifty-two. And living meant caring and loving, not buying and selling.

The selves being hammered out in tenement flats received an added dimension when the Beatles and Bob Dylan, who had their beginnings in the music of the old people, erected the framework for a new music which reflected the reality of the young, in their language and in the specifics of their experience. Rock music, it was called, and groups seemed to form whenever five white kids got together and they called themselves names which were additional ammunition against the Pentagons of the soul.

**VANILLA FUDGE**
**STRAWBERRY ALARM CLOCK**
**DOW JONES AND THE INDUSTRIALS**
**JEFFERSON AIRPLANE**
**BIG BROTHER AND THE HOLDING COMPANY**
**CHOCOLATE WATCHBAND**
**THE GRATEFUL DEAD**
**BLOOD, SWEAT AND TEARS**
**THE DOORS**

The names were surreal in the extreme, names whose meaning was not to mean. To be white in America is to be buried in a compost of meaning that means nothing because it isn't lived. The young assaulted this meaning with the techniques of a Zen master. "What is Buddha?" the monk asked the Master. "A pile of shit!" "What is enlightenment?" The Master slapped him so hard he toppled over.

With their music, they slapped America continuously. Sound became all important. Amplifiers were turned up and psychiatrists did studies proving that the music was played at such a volume that permanent damage could be done to the ear. Record jackets urged the buyers to play the records at the highest possible volume "for maximum enjoyment." While parents wondered how anyone could hear the music if it were played so loud, the young knew that the sound itself was the experience, as it is with blues and flamenco. Music was not to be listened to. It was to be touched, to be held in the pores of the skin and on the nipple of a breast. You became one with the sound and the sound became you. The music deranged the senses as did the drugs and one could perceive the world as Van Gogh had, could follow Blake's admonition and cleanse the doors of perception. Once cleansed, they opened upon a multicolored world, vibrant, living in its tiniest part. The very atoms were real.

And as they saw America for the vulgar lie it is, they began putting out their own newspapers with all the news that should be printed. Not only could they not follow their parents, they refused to believe them any longer, and in their papers they wrote of their society and the society of their parents, of their aspirations and the society's degradation. Through their newspapers and music, they came to know that they were not rebels, but members of the Lost Tribe who had found themselves and each other.

They began to like themselves for the first time and liking themselves, they liked others. Love, Love, Love. They painted their bodies to express their love and joy. They wore flowers in their hair, beads around their necks and bells around their ankles. They were breaking out of prison, but without the violence which characterized the attempts made by their counterparts in the fifties. They burned no old men. They didn't stay home from school to shoot their parents. They simply left, came together and tried to learn to love each other. Across the country during 1966 they held large gatherings which they called Be-In's (BEING) and it was like the Sermon on the Mount and everyone was Jesus. And they gave balloons to winos and flowers to policemen.

(Late one autumn night, Jean Wiley, Rap and I sat in a restaurant in Columbus Circle after going to an Odetta concert in Central Park where detectives had watched us all evening, followed us out of the park and stood outside the restaurant waiting to follow Rap home. A group of the young, flowers in their hands, walked by the window, looked in and recognized Rap. They waved and came inside.

"What's happenin'?" Rap said, in that way he can say it when he doesn't feel like saying it.

"Do you really believe in killing people?" one of them asked.

"I believe in defending my life."

"But you don't have to kill."

"Keep on believing that."

"And it's not right to hate people," another one said.

"What am I supposed to do to somebody who hates me? Kiss him?"

"Yes."

"Shit."

"But it's not right to hate people."

"Tell Lyndon Johnson to drop flowers on the Vietnamese."

"That's what he should do."

"All I know is that the Vietcong is whupping the United States' ass and they ain't doing it with flowers."

They stood there for a moment, smiling. Maybe those smiles were filled with love, but all I could feel was the pain of where they must have come from. They held out their hands and Rap shook them. Next was my turn. I looked at the outstretched hands and shook my head. Their eyes pleaded with me. Mine pleaded with them.)

The world was moving fast in 1966. In Afroamerica there was no time for flowers. Flowers were for cemeteries and cemeteries were where you went any time a white cop decided that was where you should be. The civil rights movement had pushed white youth into their initial confrontations with the society. Black Power and the urban rebellions pushed them further. Where whites were concerned about defining their lives, blacks were, too. So they went to war.

There were no generals, no regiments, no battle plans. Just some bricks, a few guns, some matches and a whole lot of anger, anger which started so far back in time that no one living could remember when it had started. It didn't start when something happened to you, but when your daddy told you what had happened to his daddy's daddy back down in Mississippi umpteen years ago. By the time it happened to you the first time, you'd already been angry for two years and you were only six. So the first time some cracker let you know that he thought you were a low-down dirty good-for-nothing nocount black-ass nigger, you were ready and just lay back and waited and one night, one of them hotass muthafucking nights when if cactus grew in the ghetto it would get up and go look for shade, one of them kind of nights when you knew the devil had turned on the air conditioning, one of them nights when you bounced a ball on the sidewalk and it didn't bounce back but just lay there and melted, one of them nights when a cop stopped some black man for doing something and somebody, nobody ever knows who the hero is, says, "Man, I'm sick and tired of this shit!" and the cop, who had arrested five hundred niggers singlehanded the week before and nothing had happened, looked up and saw a brick coming down on him that looked like it was as big as the moon and as he ducked, his prisoner jerked away and ran down the street and just as the cop reached for his gun, his motion was halted by the delicious sound of a big plate-glass window breaking and that was it! The shit had hit the fan and those who had been without were about to get. The sound of windows breaking doesn't carry around the world, but it travels mighty fast throughout the ghetto and following the religious commandment of BLESSED IS HE WHO TAKES WHAT HE WANTS AND DON'T FORGET TO DUCK, the people go shopping. Supermarketsliquorstores clothingstoresdepartmentstoresthepawnshopfurniturestorestelevisionandradiostoresandallofthemother miscellaneousstores were cleaned out quicker than a man leaving a woman's bedroom when her husband comes home unexpectedly. And then comes the best part. From somewhere somebody produces the poor man's atomic bomb, a Molotov cocktail, and with a right-hand throw worthy of a place on the starting line-up of any ballclub, it is lobbed into the now empty store and the night glows with orange flames and black smoke and the blackest of black laughter. Down the street the people run, laughing, proud, feeling good inside, while at the same time keeping an eye out for the cops, dodging bullets and sometimes failing, but always feeling like they've been reborn, not in the blood of Jesus but in the fire of retribution. The Good Book says, ye shall reap what ye sow. Lord knows the white man sho' done some sowing and it's about time black folks made him do some reaping. And reap America did. No city was safe. No city should've been.

# 2.

1967

January
Congress refuses to seat Adam Clayton Powell.
3 Astronauts die in fire.

February
*Ramparts* magazine reveals CIA funding of National Student Association.

April
Largest antiwar demonstrations to date in New York and San Francisco.

Slowly, the young began to understand. Many of them had come to "the new world" because it looked so beautiful in the LIFELOOKTIME NEWSWEEK color spreads where the girls were always more beautiful than even God could have imagined and to the young in the Great Wasteland where the Bible was read at breakfast and the whole town knew it if you didn't go to church on Sunday, Haight-Ashbury and the East Village looked better than dreams. But magazines are a reality in and of themselves which often have little relation to the reality of flesh and blood. But the young didn't know that until they came and found that the East Village was really the Lower East Side where there was no heat

Stalin's daughter defects.

May
Muhammad Ali refuses to enter the Army.

Summer
Black rebellions in more than 100 cities.

July
Stokely Carmichael visits Cuba. Rap Brown shot in Cambridge, Md.

October
Largest antiwar demonstration at Pentagon. Che murdered.

in the winter, rats, roaches, and no apartment which had not been robbed at least once. It was the sound of wine bottles smashing onto the sidewalk at two A.M. It was a three room railroad flat with the bathtub in the kitchen and a vomit-splattered commode in an unlit hallway. It was poverty Puerto Rican style and poverty black style and poverty East European style and poverty old people's style and cops on the corners and blacks on the corners playing on the guilt of white girls to get some pussy because guilty white pussy was better than no white pussy at all and it was mothers looking for daughters because they were afraid their daughters were giving up some pussy to blacks who had studied white girl psychology and graduated Phi Beta Kappa *magna cum laude* and it was white girls giving up pussy and claps and getting high and staying high and hustling tourists for money and worrying about a place to stay where they wouldn't have to give up too much pussy before they got some sleep. They came because of those color pictures, but when they got there, the pictures were all in black and white.

They began to understand and where the Beat Generation had thought of itself as white Negroes, the young of the mid-sixties stated flatly, "We are niggers." (But a haircut, shave and a suit made them white folks any day of the week they got tired of being "niggers.") Because of their long hair, clothes and psychological guerrilla warfare campaign, the police began to harass them, for what must be more infuriating to a cop than a kid who is rejecting everything he would like to have. The cop had grown up poor, his parents struggling, and when he finished high school and applied for the force, what joy there was in his house. He gained status in his neighborhood, job security and when he covered a demonstration, or walked his beat around Tompkins Square Park and saw kids who had had advantages he could barely imagine, he got angry. (It's always the older cops who beat the girls at demonstrations. They look at those girls and they think about their daughter at home, lying on the sofa reading magazines, in her micro-skirt, but what girl should have to worry about her skirt being up around her thighs in her own house when nobody's home but her father. And he wonders, the father does, what kid on the block is getting a piece of that and he can't help but wonder, the father can't, if it's good and he knows damn well it is because it's his daughter and as he realizes what he's thinking about his own daughter, his own flesh and blood, his very soul trembles and he starts yelling at his daughter for always lying around the house and not studying and how she'll never amount to anything, and the girl, stunned and hurt by the unprovoked outburst, leaves the house in anger, leaving him alone with his guilt which has turned to moral indignation about that slut of a daughter lying around with her skirt hiked up like some roadside whore and because men have never been able to admit to themselves that they'd like to fuck their own daughters, women have been burned at stakes, hung from trees, banished from towns and always locked in jails where pubic hairs are the bars and the slave owner, whom society dignifies by calling husband and father, alone has the key which never fits. And the daughters of old men wore buttons saying GO NAKED and they did when and where they could. Maybe that was what everybody needed to do for a month or so. Just go NAKED and everybody fuck everybody else. On the buses, in hallways, on the curb by the newsstands, on the subways, in the parks, on the roofs, in the elevators, on television, in the pizzeria, the delicatessen, the laundromat, EVERY-WHERE. Just walk down the street and say, "Let's fuck!" and just fuck and fuck and fuck and fuck, women fucking women, men fucking men, everybody fucking everybody else, three at a time, four at a time, undreamed of combinations and maybe after a summer of everybody going naked and fucking everybody else, then maybe America would be on the road to decency. It's hard as hell to hate somebody you've slept with. Let the John Birch Society fuck the Red Guard, an assignment which would test the revolutionary commitment of the Red Guard, not to mention the teachings of the Good Chairman. Let Fidel fuck Pat Nixon and niggers fuck everybody, which they're going to do anyway.

It wouldn't work. Somebody would stop fucking long enough to figure out how he could make money on the whole thing.)

They were not niggers, no matter how much they thought they were. But they were not what their parents wanted them to be. Many of them went back home at summer's end, heroes to the kids who had stayed behind. Some of those who returned would grow up to be hardly any different from their parents. Others would retain a small glow from their journey into America's liberated zones and although they would eventually yield to society's demands, they would quietly force society to bend a little to their demands. Many, however, never returned. It was too long a trip back. They had only the vaguest notion of where they might be going, but the mere fact of the going was enough. They knew from whence they had come and that alone was enough to keep them on their present road. (I remember walking by a construction site in Uppsala, Sweden, and as my feet touched the gravel I remembered all the gravel roads I had ever been on and the fields that surrounded them and I was painfully aware that the gravel roads of Sweden had little meaning for me. The gravel roads of the South have been impressed into the earth by black feet and black feet are my feet and walking on those roads I know that I am walking in my own footsteps. I can see the feet inside the shoes that have traveled these roads, feet with corn plasters on the toes, feet whose skin is dry and wrinkled, running feet, hurting feet, feet that need to be thrust into a bucket of hot water in front of a potbellied stove, feet that did not know shoes until they were six or seven years old, feet that have curled the mud between the toes and left their imprint in the dust.

The earth is not the same everywhere because of the feet that mold it and the hands which hold it. The earth of Western Europe is a machined earth, a rubber-tired earth, not like the earth of Spain,

Portugal, parts of Italy, not to mention Poland and
beyond. I didn't understand the earth of Sweden,
except where remains of Viking castles still stood.
Those were footsteps I could walk in.

I fell in love with mud in Vietnam. It was so
good to get out of Hanoi and walk up muddy muddy
roads in early morning mist and I could feel so
much of those fields and those people. I knew them,
because of the early morning I walked up the steep
muddy hill at Cousin Jessie's in Mississippi and it
was so muddy I slipped several times on the slip-
pery-as-ice mud and there was this mule eyeing me
rather hostilely and the rain was coming down and
I walked up the hill and climbed over a barbed wire
fence and on through a field until I came to this
sloping hill where all of my father's kin are buried
and in the distance, almost obscured by the rain,
the hills of Mississippi.

The
mud
of
Vietnam
is
woman-thigh
deep
with backs bent,
for muddiness is next to Godliness,
woman-thigh deep
in river mud at low-tide,
woman-hands
scooping mud to build
new dikes and
repair bombed ones;
woman-thigh deep

in the fields of
Hung Yen Province
carving slabs of
mud that will
be cut to
brick-size and
baked in kilns—
woman-thigh high
in water,
feet
deep
in
the
mud,
planting rice—
(with a quick
turn of the wrist
green stalks
are
thrust into the mud) ;
woman-thigh high
midst the delicate rice
hair (tied loosely
at the back of the head)
falling below the
hips
and
brushing the tops
of the
green
rice stalks.

Their
woman-ness
seems to grow from
the
mud

of
Vietnam
where they stand,
woman-thigh high,
woman-thigh deep.

I would like
to make love

woman-thigh high
woman-thigh deep

in
the
mud
of
Vietnam.

Vietnam. One cannot go there and come back the same. Particularly if you're black. To be in a country and not be surrounded by white people. What a joy. To be rid of that loneliness which comes from being constantly among a strange people who don't know anything about me and are convinced they do, a people who basically don't like me and say that they do. I look at white people and can see their little houses and lives and aspirations and it's like I don't exist. In Vietnam I felt completely free for the first time in my life, even though I couldn't talk directly to the people, didn't know the particulars of their lives and would never know them. Yet, I did know because their gentleness was mine, their mud was mine, and their enemy was mine. I did not need to hear from them, as I continually did, the facts of the war. Number killed does not mean much to me. Tonnage of bombs dropped does not move me. I know America and its capacity for evil would shame the Devil Himself. America places all of its confidence in its ability to destroy and kill and Vietnam places its confidence in people, as well it should. People are such fantastic creations, but in America we seldom have the opportunity to understand that, to feel it, to live it. But how can you destroy a people who have learned to carry a half ton of material on a bicycle, old women, old men, pushing bicycles loaded with bricks, mud, lumber and I didn't ask what else. How can you destroy a people who when a bomb is dropped in the center of their village leaving a crater thirty feet across and forty or fifty feet deep, either fill it, a bucket of dirt at a time, or simply pour water into it, a bucket at a time, and stock it with fish and then breed one and half tons of fish in the succeeding year. Driving through the city of Thanh Hoa that Easter Sunday after the planes had left for the day, I saw an old woman fishing out of a bomb crater, as if it were a lake that had been there since time immemorial. Everywhere I went in Vietnam I was given a ring made from the metal of a jet which was shot down in the area. They make medical tools from the metal of these jets. I was given a vase made from the casing of a thousand-pound bomb.

In Vietnam I learned what Man could be if given the opportunity. Even during a war, the Vietnamese exemplified a humanity I have never known. Yes, they're fighting a war, but you never forget that they are human beings fighting a war only because it has been forced upon them and if a people value themselves, they will defend themselves. In the dining room at the hotel, I flirted with the girls who waited on the tables, which isn't hard to do in Vietnam. Vietnamese women flirt outrageously, with that language of the face. One day there was an alert and we had to go to the shelter. As I went across the garden toward the bomb shelter I saw one of the waitresses running, helmet on her head, rifle in her hand, toward her position. I was stunned, because I had never dreamed that this petite young woman knew anything about guns. She felt me staring at her, I guess, because she stopped and looked at me and then blushed. Meanwhile the air raid siren is going, jets are swooping overhead, the antiaircraft guns are booming and this girl, rifle in her hand, blushes because I was staring at her. And there's no contradiction involved. Instead, that is the greatest exemplification of what it is to be revolutionary. In Vietnam I learned that the revolutionary is he who cries for those he has killed.

Revolution changes whole patterns of living and thinking. Once you get involved you start living right, as the old folks say. You know that you can't doodle on a piece of typing paper because the organization needs that piece of paper and a whole lot of people are depending on that piece of paper being used for getting out the word, not for some dude to sit up and doodle on. Once you get involved in revolution, you start to really care about people, how they feel, what they're going through and even if you can't do anything, you at least let them know that you know they're going through something and maybe that helps them endure it a little easier. But most people just throw that word around without letting it get into their lives, without letting it transform them. But the "I" which is me is more than my name, an identification tag used for social convenience. When "I" say that "I" am a revolutionary then "I" become You, if you will allow me, and You become "I." God, that's so hard. Most people won't let you inside them. We are educated to keep our "I" exclusive, to protect it and shelter it, but when we're afraid to let somebody else enter our selves, we don't live. We cling to our "I," which is like jumping from an airplane without a parachute. We cling to our "I" and like a poisonous climbing plant, it clings to us, making us so ugly, so incredibly ugly. Americans are the ugliest people in the world. Tight, hard faces. Eyes which broadcast mistrust. Beings which radiate fear of anything human. The young are different. Incredibly beautiful they are and I hope that they can retain it, let it grow. At least they're beginning to recognize that there are no institutions in the American Way of Life which encourage us to love one another and they are experimenting, trying to learn to love.

### RITUAL

Standing with her eyes closed
and her feet close together,
a young woman allowed her
limp body
to be passed slowly
from hand to hand
by four men
standing in a small circle.

"The purpose is to see
how much we are willing
to trust ourselves

and
each other,"
said the leader.

Then,
each of the five participants
walked up to the others
one at a time,
touched them on the hands
or shoulders
and told them
"what I like most about you."

(*The New York Times*—July 24, 1968)

Sometimes that learning to love takes a courage most of us can't conceive of.

### RITUAL—II

A young man
climbed over a five-foot-high fence
onto the grounds of the United Nations
last night
and
set himself on fire with gasoline.

Despite severe pain
from critical burns,
he apologized
for causing any inconvenience.

He gave no explanations of
why he had set himself afire.

(*The New York Times*—December 6, 1967)

The young are learning to love and to express that love. They are not afraid to reach out and touch another and know that that is good, that it is beautiful. It's so hard to do in America and people have to go through so many sick changes. They've been brought up to think of their bodies and feelings as ugly and no one, but no one, says anything about sex. How sick do you have to be to tell kids that a bird brought them. So once they discover their own body and someone else's body, some of them just freak out. And all they want to do is touch and feel and feel and touch. They can't get enough.

GREEK male, 25, good-looking, clean cut and congenial, seeks attractive and clean female who enjoys to be sexually satisfied by oral stimulation. Call ——— day preferable.

SAVAGELY hung black male, 27, seeks passionate white female. Have own pad and car. Don't be shy. Write ———

INTELLIGENT and attractive afro-american, well hung 8 inches, seeks gay men to suck his cock and suck his ass. Send address and telephone number. Please hurry. ———

THREE students, 2 chicks, 1 guy, want well hung guys and stacked chicks for gang bangs. If you fuck, suck, or take it up the ass, send sexy picture and address. ———

(*East Village Other*—January 31, 1969)

But when you've been out in the cold all day, you want to get as close to the fire as possible when you come inside. The next generation will be much more casual, because this generation established the base camp.

Young blacks laugh at the struggles of young whites to free themselves. Yes, it is pathetic to read the ads in underground papers where people advertise for somebody to fuck and I would laugh, too, except for all the pain of loneliness which is really being advertised. And yes, I know, too, that those young whites are not free from racism, but at least they are conscious of so much that their parents have never known. Above all I know that those young whites can not be completely trusted. They can choose to go back home at any minute. But I want to trust them, to believe in them. They, too, are human and I do not want to do to them what has been done to me. I can't ask other blacks, however, to forego the pleasure of hating. A part of me hates also. Sometimes, all of me, because they will never know, those young white kids, what it is like and I want to drown them in their whiteness. But, because they cannot completely know is no reason to deny them their right to humanity. They, too, are human and those I can love, I do and only hope that their numbers multiply with the rising of each sun.)

# five

# 1.

1968

January
King plans
march on
Washington.
Philip Blai-
berg receives
a new heart.
*Pueblo* seized.
Tet offensive.

February
Battle of Hue.
Mia Farrow
consults Ma-
harishi.
Nixon starts

Nineteen sixty-eight began with the murder of Che. On the calendar it was the autumn of 1967 (but what do calendars know of changes in the soul). It was impossible to believe Che was dead. We wanted to believe that another of Dean Rusk's fantasies had gotten into the papers. Then came the photographs of a half-naked Che lying on a table looking too incredibly like Jesus. The young, however, refused to believe the photographs until Fidel confirmed that they were all too true. (Che was still

campaign.
Romney quits
campaign.
Siege of
Khesanh.

**March**
Kerner Com-
mission Re-
port.
Dollar
threatened.
McCarthy al-
most defeats
Johnson in
New Hampshire
primary.
Kennedy en-
ters race.
Johnson with-
draws.

**April**
King murdered.
125 cities
go up.
46 killed.
2600 injured.
21,000 ar-
rested.
Rudi Dutchke
shot in Ger-
many.
Columbia
University
revolt.
Humphrey and
Rockefeller
decide to run.

**May**
Paris Revolt.
Poor People's

alive when Stokely, George Ware and I were in Cuba the summer of 1967. There were huge billboards in Havana and Santiago with his picture and those words of his: "The duty of a revolutionary is to make the revolution." Everyday there were rumors that Che was coming to appear at the meeting of the Organization of Latin American Solidarity which we were attending. But he didn't. Twice I saw Che's wife, not that it meant anything. If she hadn't been pointed out to me, I wouldn't have noticed her from any other Cuban woman. I couldn't help but wonder, though, what she really thought of Che, who was hardly ever at home, even when he was in Cuba. It was probably hard being Mrs. Che. Maybe she understood, though, how hard it was to be Che.) If Fidel said that Che was dead, then he was. Fidel would not lie.

The young held meetings to commemorate the life of Che and excoriate the United States for his death. Posters of him were printed and they tacked his image over their beds and over their desks. A previous generation had wept at the death of James Dean, a symbol of self-destruction, of rebellion without content. Che was a cosmogony in and of himself. He had died as a midwife to the New Man.

The murder of Che only intensified the revolutionary fervor of the young. The United States could kill a man named Ernesto Guevara, but from his death would come hundreds of thousands more Guevaras. However, the would-be Che's were far from being the revolutionary Che had been. It didn't matter. If they didn't yet know how a revolution was fought and won, they were at least able to express their total hatred of what now existed and that was a beginning on which others could build. Just as Che knew that he could not model himself after anyone, they would learn the same. They could learn from Che. They could not be him. They could emulate Che (a far more admirable endeavor than emulating one's father), and to have Che as a reference point in one's life, to have Che as an internal monitor, scrutinizing every thought and every action, could only be considered good.

The Cubans called 1968 "The Year of the Heroic Guerrilla" in memory of Che and in recognition of the guerrillas around the world who were fighting and dying. America's guerrillas were preparing for their battles, because 1968 was to be the year

John Carlos protest at Olympics. Bombing of North Vietnam stopped.

November
Nixon wins. Catholics protest against Pope's encyclical.

December
Trip around moon. Julie and David marry. Mideast. Pueblo crew released.

they would shake the empire. Some even hoped, in their naïveté, to bring it down.

Nineteen sixty-eight was a presidential election year and as such, it held out the prospect for change. Every four years, the democratic rhetoric tells us, we have the opportunity to let our wishes be known as to whom we think should run the government. Every four years, the rhetoric tells us, we can exercise that most precious of political privileges and responsibilities and enter a booth and cast our ballot. Every four years, the voice and will of the people can make itself heard and felt.

That was what they taught in fifth grade civics, but the young knew it wasn't true. They were not a part of the political process. No American was. Votes were necessary for appearance's sake, but the will of the people exists in a domain separate from the center of power and the latter, in the interests of self-preservation, would never allow itself to be affected by the former. The faces in the White House change; the political labels change, but the acts and attitudes emanating from the White House don't. Anyone who occupies the White House accepts the rules of the game without question; each simply thinks that he can deal the cards better than another. Elections merely choose the dealer.

The youth wanted a new game. Some politicians recognized that the disaffection of youth with the political process had gone beyond the danger point and one of them, Eugene McCarthy, sought, by running for President, to bring the young back into the system, to prove to them that the machinery could serve them, too. Needless to say, he failed. His surprising showing in the New Hampshire primary, however, forced Robert Kennedy to declare himself a candidate. (Kennedy intimates claim that this is not so. If Fidel had said it wasn't so, we would believe it. Until Fidel does . . .) By waiting until McCarthy had shown that there was a possibility of defeating Johnson, Kennedy couldn't help but look like an opportunist. And everyone knew that he'd been waiting since the death of his brother to go after Johnson's ass.

Lyndon Johnson, however, decided to deny Bobby the pleasure. He withdrew from the race with many platitudes and much bullshit. In the process, however, he endeared himself to the American people and received a measure of that love he had wanted so desperately for five years. Johnson wanted to be an heroic figure. He had sought to bring the nation together and all of his efforts at consensus only split the nation more. The consensus was that Americans hated him for practically any reason one could think of. But by withdrawing from the race, Johnson suddenly became a tragic figure. He was a man stepping down from power for the sake of his country, the newspaper editors and TV commentators wanted us to believe. But the young knew and in New York, they ran through the streets shouting the glorious news. They knew that they were the ones who had made Lyndon Johnson pack his bags. Now the job was to make all of them pack their bags.

## THE CANDIDATE—I

Mrs. McCarthy
told the women
that her husband
had a strong civil rights voting record
and
that during her trip
with him
to
the
funeral of the
Rev.
Dr.
Martin Luther King, Jr.,
they got
the feeling
"that good
will
eventually
triumph."

(*The New York Times*—April 12, 1968)

## THE  CANDIDATE—II

Senator Kennedy
is
speaking
more
and
more
in the
higher  tones,
and
there
is a
strong

emotional
content
in his words.

At night
he
says,
"Here,
while the moon shines,
our
brave
young
men
are dying
in the swamps
of
Vietnam."

During the day
he
says,
"Here,
while the sun shines,
our
brave
young
men
are dying
in the swamps
of
Southeast Asia."

(*The New York Times*—March 25, 1968)

As gratified as the young were that their efforts
had not gone unrewarded, they could not take all of
the credit. In fact, most of the congratulations had
to go to the Vietcong, who made it obvious that the

only way the United States could win was to transform Vietnam into a graveyard. In January of
1968, the NLF unleashed what has come to be known
as the Tet offensive, during which they attacked
over one hundred towns, villages and military in-
stallations in one night and continued their offensive
for several weeks. They attacked Saigon itself, and
almost succeeded in getting inside the U.S. Embassy.
The Tet offensive proved conclusively who was in
control of the war. The United States could do
nothing more than react as best it could whenever
the NLF chose to act. Everybody knew that one
does not win a war by reacting.

The Western world hit upon what might be the
answer to losing wars when a South African honky
had his heart removed and replaced with the heart
of a black man. Transplanting organs was the logical extension of capitalism, where man is defined
quantitatively and materialistically. The quality of
a man's life has never been a concern of Western
society despite its many-spired cathedrals. (I stood
on the Left Bank of the Seine and looked at Notre
Dame for a long time, visualizing how it was
erected, stone by stone, and the mortar turned to
the coagulated blood of those whose lives were
represented by those stones. How obscene to offer
a building to God when it is our Being we should
offer. But we erect buildings and temples to escape
the terrifying task of letting God use our voices and
our tongues to speak. Notre Dame would have to be
destroyed, too, because it separated Man from himself.) The West assumes, without question, that a
long life is a good life. There is no relationship
between the two and when one looked at the photo-

graphs of Philip Blaiberg, it was legitimate to ask why he should live beyond the time his heart would've allowed him. Indeed, a glance at his fat, stupid face made one wonder if his heart had not been negligently kind to have allowed him to live this long. The West went on an orgy of transplanting hearts and anything else in the body which wasn't nailed down.

### THE PROVIDER

An
eleven-year-old boy
from Loma Linda, Calif.,
died
last week
of
auto-accident injuries.
Within the day,
his
kidneys
were transplanted into two men,
an extract from his spleen
was injected into a leukemia patient,
and
surgeons used
some of his skin
as grafts
for a severely burned woman.

(*Time*—May 10, 1968)

Was there anything good which could be said for a society which would spend $40,000 to perform a heart transplant and at the same time allow a family to be evicted from their home for nonpayment of rent? Was there anything good which could be said for a society which would wait until a man had a terminal illness and then take extreme measures to save his life but would be totally indifferent to the man who could not afford to go to a doctor. (For five and a half years Joan and I lived in a subbasement on West 21st Street. We had to keep the lights on day and night; there were roaches; there were rats. In the winter, there were many days without heat. The building had no superintendent, so we put the garbage out on the street and the cats and rats would tear at the sacks, turn them over, and the garbage would spill into the doorway. The ceiling in the kitchen was falling. Every winter morning we would awake to the overpowering stench of rats, live ones and dead ones, coming up from the basement. Occasionally, a rat would die in the walls of the apartment and somehow, I would find it and get it out. Both of our children were conceived there, on the bed in the living room. After Jody was born, I spent the days before she and Joan came home filling the cracks in the wall with steel wool to keep out the rats, spraying with insecticide to kill the roaches and scrubbing the floors and walls. Our first-born was coming home. We brought her home, placed her in the crib and put a net over it. That was to keep the roaches off her. I sat up at night, all night for the first week, beside her so that the rats wouldn't come. But she got sick the first day she was home and stayed sick for nine months. The doctor said she was allergic to her mother's milk, which is like fish being allergic to water. What do doctors know? How can you tell what is wrong with somebody if you don't know where they live? The doctor said my ulcer came from tension and he told me I should relax. He was so confident as he said it. I wanted to scream at him, Muthafucka, do you know what it is to be so cold for months and months, to be so cold that all you can think of is the sun? Do you know what it is to be afraid to take a shit because you're afraid the rats will come out of the holes in the wall next to the stool, to be afraid to shit for five-and-a-half years! I knew that my ulcer would disappear if the doctor would exchange apartments with me.

I went to Mississippi. Not because of any of that, but I had work to do and one Sunday night, Joan called. She was hysterical. She had heard a noise in Jody's room and had gone in to find a rat beneath her crib. She woke Jody up and could find no scratches or bite marks on her. I wanted to kill somebody. The Mayor? But it really wasn't his fault. The Governor? Killing him wouldn't get the rats out. There was no one individual I could kill and know that it would mean the end to the rats and roaches and crumbling walls in every apartment and house in every city. Everything had to be changed— the way people thought, the way people saw, heard, felt and breathed. This system had taught us to accept the existence of rats. Our lives had to grow from different soil.

Our second-born, Malcolm Coltrane, was six weeks premature and I refused to bring him home from the hospital for the first month. They wanted to send him home after a week. He would've died in that apartment. So he stayed where it was clean, he stayed and got strong, so that when he came home and began crawling around the floor squashing roaches and showing them to us, it wouldn't matter.

Eventually, we were accepted into a housing project and I was delirious with joy, but couldn't forget that there were still so many people on West 21st Street and they were there for the same reason we had been there. They didn't have the money to be anywhere else. People suffer and people die because they don't have the money to be anywhere else.

Revolutionaries are not born. They are made by living on West 21st Street. The United States has made more revolutionaries than Che Guevara ever did. The slaveholder trains his own executioners.)

Only a dying culture would seek to save itself by feeding upon its dead. Only a dying culture would exult about putting some men on the moon while half of mankind lives on the starvation level. The moon will always be there, but each person who lives has barely an instant and most of the world's people are never able to know that instant. In a society where life had meaning beyond the beating of the heart, the ability to transplant organs would be an occasion for celebration. In a society where man had within his grasp the ability to be Man, a trip to the moon would be awesome. In the West, all of it is obscene.

# 2.

There was no spring in 1968. The winds of winter died as our northern half of the world tilted toward the sun, but there was no spring. April was scarcely old enough to know its name when Martin Luther King was hurled into Death. (I was sitting on the toilet when Joan yelled, "King's been shot!" I had no reaction. Black people had been getting shot all my life and I accepted it as one of the facts of life. A few minutes later she came to the door and told me that he was dead. I didn't react. I hadn't loved him and there was no point in pretending otherwise. I turned the radio off and turned on the TV, figuring that one of the networks undoubtedly would be showing an instant replay in slow motion. Instead, there was the terror-filled voice of a white newscaster who knew that white folks had just lost their best friend. I could hear them thinking that of all the niggers to shoot, King should've been on the bottom of the list. There were a thousand militant, dangerous niggers around that needed to be shot. Yeah, it was obvious that white folks had messed up but good this time. Then Lyndon Johnson came on and he looked like he'd just seen the Vietcong sneaking up the back lawn. It was obvious that he was going to use all that bullshit rhetoric to tell niggers to please not burn down his country. ". . . We can achieve nothing by lawlessness and divisive-

ness among the American people. It's only by joining together, and only by working together, can we
continue to move toward equality and fulfillment for
all of our people. I hope that all Americans tonight
will search their hearts as they ponder this most
tragic incident." Then I reacted and I was angry.
Black people die and the government covers the
grave with bullshit.)

King's corpse was not cold before blacks turned
night into day. They knew that the bullet had killed
a little of each of them. For ten days blacks "joined
together" and "worked together" and the smoke
from the purifying flames even drifted over the
White House in huge, black billows.

(I debated with myself about going to the funeral
and was sorry afterwards that I hadn't. At least I
would've been among black people all that day and
it would've been a purgation of some kind. I found,
to my surprise, in the days following the assassination that I had loved him and I felt guilty that I
had let my disagreements choke that love until he
was no longer alive to disagree with. So I watched
his funeral on television. All day I sat there and
it only served to increase my anger as I saw
McCarthy, Kennedy, Nixon and the rest of their
kind enter the church. It was the social event
of the spring that never was. And Dr. King was
laid to rest without one of those good Baptist funerals which he knew how to preach, those funerals
where the preacher knows you want to cry have to
cry just gotta cry, Lord, and he knows what chords
in the soul to play to make the tears come pouring
down your face, the sobs to choke in your throat.
He knows that you don't want a lecture, a speech, a

lot of platitudes. You want to scream and fall out
in a dead faint as they carry the casket up the aisle.
GOOD GOD! He knows that you want to throw
yourself on top of the casket and scream, CARRY
ME AWAY, TOO, LORD! I AIN'T GOT NO BUSI-
NESS STAYIN' HERE AND HIM GONE! The
preacher knows all about HELP ME, JESUS, cause
Death ain't got no mercy. It stings like whiplashes
on water-drenched flesh. It's a hurting which just
coils up inside and jabs you for months and months.
Naw, they didn't do Dr. King right. They talked
over his body, but they didn't lay him away like he
was supposed to be laid away. He was the biggest
nigger in the country and the funeral should've gone
on for two days at least.

Mrs. King knew and that's why she had them
play a tape of one of his sermons, 'cause when you
come right down to it, there really wasn't anybody
who could've preached King's funeral right except
King himself.

### FUNERAL ORATION

If any of you are around
when I have to meet my day,
I don't want a long funeral.
And if you get somebody
to deliver the eulogy
tell him not to talk too long.
Tell him not to mention
that I have a Nobel Peace Prize—
that isn't important.
Tell him not to mention
that I have 300 or 400 other awards—
that's not important.

Tell him not to mention
where I went to school.

I'd like somebody to mention that day
that
Martin Luther King, Jr.,
tried to give his life serving others.

I'd like somebody to say that day
that
Martin Luther King, Jr.,
tried to love somebody.

I want you to say that day
that I tried to be right
and to walk with them.

I want you to be able to say that day
that I did try
to feed the hungry.
I want you to be able to say that day
that I did try in my life
to visit those who were in prison.
And I want you to say
that I tried to love and serve
humanity.

Yes,
if you want to,
say that I was a drum major.
Say that I was a drum major for justice.
Say that I was a drum major for peace.
Say that I was a drum major for righteousness.

(*Jet*—April 18, 1968)

Amen. Amen.)

Martin Luther King, Jr., called upon black people

to be as Christian as Christ. It was an unreasonable demand. To hate was the natural human response to being hated. The white man taught blacks to hate him and there was no question of loving whites until they appeared to be worthy of love. Dr. King's concept of love as a political weapon had some meaning within the walls of the black church which had always preached that there was no higher calling than to love one's enemy. But any church which takes a dead man nailed to a wooden cross as its central symbol is capable of articulating all kinds of sicknesses. It was the symbolism of King which blacks responded to and loved. The one hundred and twenty-five cities which blacks turned into funeral pyres were proof enough that King's personal philosophy could not successfully be used politically. Martin talked like us, but he thought like them. They mourned him, for it was in him that they found absolution. We vindicated him, for it was in his death that we learned, beyond a doubt, that if he, who offered nothing but love, could be murdered, then the lives of us lesser blacks were that much more precarious.

MARTYRS AND VICTIMS OF THE SEARCH
FOR THE NEW LAND
*Chicago—April, 1968*

CURTIS JEFRO
31 years old
a die caster
lived in a housing project.
He went out on his
12th-floor balcony
to observe a disturbance.

He was found dead
of a wound
that the police
attributed to a stray bullet.

MARVIN CARTER
24
married with three children
was to have started a new job.
He left home around 5 P.M.
Four hours later
the police saw
some men carrying merchandise
from a South Side store.
They fired
and Mr. Carter
fell dead
in an alley.

ROBERT T. DORSEY
31
a truck driver
and his wife
were walking home
when shots rang out.
Mr. Dorsey pushed his wife
to the ground,
then fell,
moaning,
"They got me.
They shot me
in my back."

PONOWEL HOLLOWAY,
16,
was shot
and killed

by the police
while he was looting a store.
He was a sophomore
at Marshall High School.

JOHN SANDIFER,
24,
bled to death
in a gutter,
apparently from a
huge gash in his knee.
The police said
he might have been
a looter
who cut himself
on a broken window in a looted store.

ERNEST MCINTYRE
20
a Negro janitor,
was looting
a liquor store
when shot by a policeman,
the police say.

HAROLD BENTLEY,
34,
a Negro construction worker,
was killed
when a wall of a
smoldering brick building
collapsed
on him.

AN UNIDENTIFIED NEGRO BOY,
about 14,
was found
dead

in the charred ruins
of a variety store.

GEORGE W. NEELY,
18,
a junior at a vocational school
was also
found dead
in the store's ruins.

WILLIAM V. STEPTER
47
was shot
by a city policeman
as he ran from a tavern.
The police listed him as
a looter.

ALBERT D. MILLER
21
was shot
by the police
in a gunfight.

ROBERT VAUGHAN,
18
was being searched
along with some other youths
suspected of looting
when he backed up into
the drawn gun of a
white policeman
and the
gun
ac-
ci-
dent-
ally discharged.

JAMES F. MURRAY
25
a white management trainee
was shot
as he walked near his home.
The police arrested
CLARENCE C. UNDERWOOD
27
and charged him with first-degree homicide.
Detectives said
Mr. Underwood's wife had told them
he left the house after Dr. King's death,
saying,
"My king is dead.
I'm going out and get me a honkie."

(*The New York Times*—April 13, 1968)

For the death of Martin Luther King, America
knew that it stood condemned, but instead of being
goaded into significant action by its guilt, America
continued to arm itself for any future black uprisings
and magazines were filled with articles detailing the
virtues of Mace, the Stoner Gun, Instant Banana
Peel and various gases that could be used against
blacks. America knew that it had within its midst
an alien and hostile minority of some thirty million
people. If they could not be controlled, there was
always the final solution and America was getting
a lot of practice in Vietnam.

But it was recognized that there were other things
which could be done before such a "regrettable"
step would have to be taken. The committee which
President Johnson had appointed to analyze the
urban rebellions turned in a report which charged
America with racism and stated that the country

was moving toward two separate societies. When has America not been two separate societies? But the Kerner Commission, as the President's committee was called, was not as concerned about historical accuracy as it was in dealing with the situation and it became clear that America had to move quickly to assimilate enough of Afroamerica to defuse it. The Commission recommended a massive domestic Marshall Plan, which was immediately ignored by the Government.

Nonetheless, some sectors of America got the message and if the Government did not move to solve the problems, some people at least felt that they could buy time if they made blacks feel better. Overnight, black people suddenly saw people who looked like them on their television screens. After a while it was well-nigh impossible to turn on the television set and not see a nigger. Niggers were talking about how good they felt in the morning after drinking V-8 juice after they had brushed their teeth with either the NEW MINT-flavored Crest or REGULAR-flavored Crest. Niggers were driving to work in Dodges and filling up at Sunoco. Niggers with Afros and dashikis were smoking Newport cigarettes and NBC's situation comedy "Julia," was the number one program in the nation. There were nigger cowboys riding across the plains, nigger undercover agents, niggers in space and it was supposed to make the niggers in hell feel that things weren't so bad. It was merely an extension of the kind of thinking which twenty years ago told blacks that things were getting better because there was a Negro Federal Judge and a Negro baseball player. Things were supposed to be getting better because you could sit behind a desk at Chase Manhattan with a twelve-foot high Afro and a dashiki made by Jomo Kenyatta's grandmama. Meanwhile, the fire trucks were still rushing through the cold winter streets to tenement houses set afire by faulty boilers and you still faced the same possibility of psychic destruction when you had to deal with a white person.

A new black organization, The Black Panther Party, was in the community, trying to relate to the brother and sister on the block and they looked tough coming down the street in their black berets and black leather jackets and their forthright adherence to the gun as the way to liberation. Eldridge Cleaver was their chief spokesman and with his book, *Soul On Ice,* he became a celebrity. White people dug him, because he fit into that literary category that made Jean Genet and Francois Villon celebrities. America does not expect faggots, thieves and ex-convicts to be articulate. Cleaver was an ex-con ("A rapist!") and liberal white America came in its pants behind it all. Cleaver was turned into a public personality and revolutions need revolutionaries, not personalities. With their uniforms and rhetoric, the Panthers attracted too much attention and Huey Newton was given thirteen years, Bobby Hutton was killed, Cleaver had to go into exile to keep from going back to jail, Bobby Seale was indicted on a Federal charge and in one week, the grapevine said, two hundred fifty Panthers across the country were arrested on various, trumped-up charges. The Black Panthers were like the rattlesnake (an American reptile), shaking their rattles before they struck. They should've been like the python (an African reptile), camouflaged among the leaves, striking silently and swiftly and returning to shelter to wait and strike again (silently and swiftly).

Afroamerica constituted a constant threat, but because it lacked leaders (Stokely married Miriam Makeba and split the country), that threat was lessened. Everybody agreed that black is beautiful, but black meant too many things and America moved quickly to try and make it possible to be black and enter the system. The effort was doomed to failure, but how long the failure would take was the unanswerable question.

However long it took would be too long, but revolutions proceed, not by the intensity of one's desires, but by their own laws. The revolutionary's duty is to know that what to do can never be separated from when to do. There is, however, always something to do.

# six

# 1.

DEATH OF A HERO

i

Waiting for him
in the serving pantry
was a small,
swarthy,
bristly haired man,
dressed all in blue,
one hand concealed
in a rolled-up Kennedy poster,
a faint smile flickering.

Kennedy emerged from a connecting corridor.
Spying the kitchen help
lined up to the left of his path,

he fell into a sidewise shuffle
and began to shake hands.
Ethel was separated
from him in the crush.
He turned
to look
for her.

The little man in blue
darted toward him.
The hand came out
of the rolled-up poster,
in it a .22 caliber
Iver-Johnson Cadet revolver.
Slowly,
almost studiedly,
the little man
pulled the trigger.
The gun went
*pop!*
then a pause,
then
*pop!*

And there lay
Robert Kennedy,
42 years old,
flat on his back,
his arms out,
his legs slightly bent,
his eyes now shut,
now open
and staring
sightlessly into some private distance.

Ethel Kennedy
moved helplessly
at the edge of the crush,

near tears of frustration,
begging for help
until spectators propelled her
over the crowd
to her husband.

She dropped to her knees
at his side,
crooning to him.
"Give him air,
please give him air,"
Mrs. Kennedy pleaded.
Once, she jumped up
shouting and waving
at the photographers.
"Get them out,
get them out!"
she cried.
A cameraman yelled back,
"This is history, lady,"
and
the flashguns kept flaring.

## ii

### at the hospital

A too-eager news photographer
tried to
barge in
and got knocked to the floor by Bill Barry.
A Guard attempted to keep
both a priest and Ethel
away from the emergency room,
flashed a badge,
which Ethel knocked from his hand.
The guard struck at her;

Tuck and Fred Dutton swept him aside.
Then the priest
was allowed
to administer
extreme unction.

(*Time*—June 14, 1968)

The wheel within the wheel within the wheel spun
us all into a reality which was too much of a *deus
ex machina* for even a Sophocles or a Mississippi
blues singer. He who had eulogized his brother was
now being eulogized. He who had carried the coffin,
marched in the funeral procession and stood beside
the grave was now being washed by the under-
taker's unfeeling sponges, dressed and the lid of
the coffin closed because no one should see what
happens when a bullet explodes inside the brain.


iii

the burial

Along the lamplit streets,
past a luminescence of
sad
and
silent faces,
the cavalcade wound through the federal city
and across the Potomac,
where in a green grove up the hill in Arlington,
John Kennedy's grave
looks out over the
city
and
the river.

The moon,
the slender candles,
the eternal flame at John's memorial—
47 feet away—
and the floodlights
laved
Robert Kennedy's
resting place beneath a magnolia tree.
It was 11 o'clock,
the first night time burial at Arlington in memory.
There was no playing of taps,
no rifle volley.
After a brief and simple service,
the coffin flag was folded into a triangle
for presentation to Ethel,
and the band played
*America the Beautiful.*

(*Time*—June 16, 1968)

## iv

### the nation in mourning

On the national day of mourning
for Robert F. Kennedy,
promotors of a Davenport, Iowa,
pistol-shooting match
decided to go ahead with the event,
but to observe a
moment
of
silence
after each volley,
out of respect
to the assassinated
Senator.

(*Time*—June 21, 1968)

In death, the Kennedy brothers and Martin Luther King became a holy trinity (and even I could not stop the tears from suffusing my eyes when I saw the photographs of the three widows—Jackie, Coretta and Ethel). But they were only the luminaries in a mob of martyrs during the decade of assassinations—Herbert Lee, William Moore, Medgar Evers, Chaney, Goodman and Schwerner, three unidentified portions of bodies fished from Mississippi rivers during the search for Chaney, Goodman, and Schwerner, Rev. James Reeb, Viola Liuzzo, Jonathan Daniels, Jimmie Lee Jackson, Malcolm X, Lee Harvey Oswald, Sammy Younge, Jr., Vernon Dahmer and Bobby Hutton. America asked itself, who's next?

### FATHER

> A Detroit man
> heard footsteps in his home,
> saw the knob of his
> bedroom door
> open slowly,
> levelled his
> bedside pistol
> and
> fatally drilled
> his three-year-old daughter
> through the head.

(*Time*—June 21, 1968)

The President dutifully appointed a committee to look into the matter of violence. At the same time, he sent a gun control bill to Congress and fought hard for its passage. If he'd been serious, he would've dusted off some old law from somewhere that would've given him the power to close down the weapons and ammunition factories. Not that it would've mattered. An American can be alone on a raft in the middle of the ocean and if it's necessary, come up with a gun from somewhere. If the President had in any way been serious about eliminating violence from America, his first step would have been an unconditional cessation of the war. (It will probably take Vietnam a generation before its air is free of the odor of gunpowder.) The President could see no relationship between domestic violence and international violence.

The assassination of the younger Kennedy afforded psychologists a golden opportunity to pull out their old college term papers linking violence and television watching and these were dutifully published by one and all and television network officials decided that they would eliminate some of the violence from their programming. They failed to recognize that violence on television was an outlet, not an impetus toward violence. You can sit and watch a Western and with the agonized cry of each victim, the fall of each body, you are a little more cleansed of the violence you had restrained yourself from inflicting upon your friends at work, your boss, your kids and your wife and husband. Take violence off television and each day in every city will be a gunfight at the O.K. Corral.

Violence was defined as a bullet in the brain and unrecognized was the fact that this kind of violence was only a manifestation of the violence done to the soul which made the young talk incessantly of Love and carry flowers. The report of a rifle is all too obviously violent, while the violence done to the soul has no sound, but if one looks closely into the faces passing on the street, its effects are unmistakeable. They are faces that can scream JUMP! at someone on a hotel window ledge, faces so strangled with fear that they will give no more than a glance to someone lying on a sidewalk. It is the violence of "If I have but one life to live, let me live it as a blonde." It is the violence of air pollution so pervasive that infants in carriages are brought inside with flakes of soot in their hair and on their faces. The bombing of Hiroshima was the logical extension of the New York City subway system.

Violence has no relationship to guns and passing laws to control the ownership of weapons will not stop violence. In Vietnam and Cuba, citizens carry rifles and pistols throughout the course of each day. Yet, there are no gun battles in the streets of Hanoi or Havana. While America's leaders travel in bullet-proof limousines with armed bodyguards running alongside, Fidel and Ho Chi Minh walk the streets and roads of their countries as they please. In fact, it is easier for a Cuban to kill the leaders of his country than it is for an American to shake his leader's hand. If we live in fear of each other, is it any wonder that we live in fear of the world?

# 2.
***

There was no spring, but even if there had been, few would have noticed. Spring is for the young, the poets have told us. It is a time to fall in love and stock up memories for those years when the past is one's all-pervading reality. In the spring of 1968, some of the young fell in love behind the barricaded doors of buildings on the campus of Columbia University. Five buildings were occupied and the police were eventually used to remove the students. The police did so with their customary attentiveness to the fine details of groin-kicking, head-smashing, hair-pulling and dragging people down steps in such a way that they would know for the rest of their lives just how many steps there were leading from Low Library. White liberals were enraged by the brutality of the arrests, but the police could not have acted otherwise being who they are. They didn't understand what people were upset about. They hadn't killed anybody. Only tried to knock some sense into their heads.

The uprising at Columbia was barely worthy of mention, however, when the birds of May brought the Paris uprising. Tactically and theoretically, the students of Paris were more advanced than the American students. They barricaded streets, not buildings, with cars and paving stones and some of their barricades looked like the walls of medieval castles. From behind their bastions, they fought, night after night, transporting themselves back to the days of *Liberté, Egalité, Fraternité*. The average Frenchman joined in at various phases of the fighting, because it appealed to his sense of history. The Paris Uprising involved the young and the workers to a degree that almost toppled the government of Charles De Gaulle. However, *mon Général* survived, much to everyone's surprise, except his. He knew better than anyone perhaps, Lenin's dictum that revolution is only possible when the government is no longer able to govern (among other things). The young could take over college buildings, the streets, even stop the economy for a few days, but the government was far from being unable to govern.

The American government was shaken in 1968 as it hadn't been in recent memory. For the young, 1968 was to have been the year it was shaken asunder. From the beginning of the year, it was obvious that the Democratic Convention in Chicago was to be the arena for the big confrontation. Johnson, Humphrey and the Democratic Party had come to be the preeminent symbols for the evil of America. The Democratic Convention was also to have a confrontation within its ranks between those who sought an identity with the young and the party "regulars." With the death of Robert Kennedy, the general who was to have led the troops was no more. Eugene McCarthy lacked the necessary charisma and by the time the convention opened, it seemed that Hubert Horatio Humphrey was going to win the nomination without too much opposition in the ranks. For those of us for whom cynicism is the only weapon we can use to preserve a modicum of sanity in America's daily descent toward death, it was not too much to superimpose over the newspaper photographs of the second slain Kennedy, a picture of a laughing Hubert Humphrey. As unseemly as it might be, surely when Humphrey heard the news, he must've thought how that improved his possibilities of getting the nomination.

August came and throughout the city of Chicago, the police, National Guard and Army stood by to deal with the young. Blacks in Chicago and around the nation knew a set-up when they saw one and they knew that if one black man let his match burn too long while igniting a cigarette one night, it would be the excuse "the man" was looking for to move his fire power into the black community and kill some black people. So all those blacks who couldn't manage to get back down South to visit Grandmother just became invisible and totally apolitical. "You say there's a Democratic Convention in town? Is that one of them new extra-long cigarettes?" "Chicago? You mean to say that this here is Chicago? No wonder it don't look like St. Louis." The Democratic Convention didn't exist in Chicago's black community.

Although the threat to the public tranquility did not come from the black community as many might have expected, that threat did come in the reaction of Chicago's police to the young.

## CHICAGO—AUGUST, 1968

Now
the waiting police were eager to move.
Some youths fled from the park.
Most stayed.

The police then lobbed
canisters of tear gas into the barricade.
Coughing,
gagging,
and
stumbling, the demonstrators broke
and ran,
some throwing stones as they retreated.
Members of the Chicago police's elite Task Force Unit
raced after the kids,
and in the darkness of the park,
ran scores of them to the ground
like cowboys bull-dogging cattle.
The sound of night sticks
smashing into skulls
resounded through the park,
mixed with shrieks and screams.
"Oh, no!"
"Oh, my God!"
"No, no, no!"
A teen-aged girl lay on the ground as
two policemen bent over her
and
beat her on the head
until her screams
faded
into a
sobbing moan.

(*Newsweek*—September 9, 1968)

Not only were the young victims of the police at-
tacks, but the press was systematically chosen by
the night sticks and Mace cans. Eventually the police
carried their offensive to the headquarters of Eugene McCarthy on the 15th floor of the Conrad

Hilton Hotel where they bloodied the bright-eyed, ever-clean-for-Gene kids.

(The slaughter on Michigan Avenue came the night of Humphrey's nomination. As a radio newsman covering the Convention, I was in the crowd in front of the Hilton. It was a happy crowd of young kids going to be slaughtered. What I had missed at the Pentagon I would see in Chicago, but I didn't want to now. Many of them had tear gas masks slung over their shoulders. Those who knew medicine or were young doctors and nurses had on their white jackets and everytime I saw one, I thought of vultures. Everyone accepted the fact that they were going to be brutalized and they were prepared to have their wounds mended. I looked around for anyone who had come to fight and saw no one. I thought of what the scene would've been like had it been five thousand blacks coming down the street and I knew that the night air would be jagged with the sound of windows breaking. But these were white kids and many of them were carrying signs: CHICAGO IS PRAGUE. They were white kids, who could be outraged by the so-called Russian invasion of Czechoslovakia. During the Republican Convention in Miami, several blacks had been killed during an uprising in the black community. But it was still easier for white kids to become enraged by something halfway around the world than next door. Chicago was not Prague. Chicago was Chicago. But they carried their signs and the only time during the night when I felt any excitement was when, all of a sudden, the entire throng of five thousand began shouting, FUCK LYNDON! FUCK LYN-

DON! FUCK LYNDON! For a minute or so, they chanted it and it was exhilarating, to say the least.

A few minutes later I felt the crowd in front of me begin to move and looking down the street I saw the police marching toward us in rows of six, at least four deep, holding their clubs horizontally down in front of them. Having no aspirations toward being a prize-winning newsman, it took me less than an instant to decide that no broadcast was worth a drop of my blood and I, along with the scant few other blacks in the crowd, split. I returned to my hotel room, a short block away from the Hilton, turned on NBC and saw in living color the images to match the screams I could hear coming from the street.

The next morning I got up early and walked through Grant Park, which is directly across from the Hilton. Many of the kids had slept there and were still sleeping as I meandered through the park. The National Guard lined the sidewalk on the park side of Michigan Avenue, but the young paid them little attention. Some played guitars; others waded and bathed and played in the fountain. Most just lay in the sun and despite my bitterness at their naïveté the night before, they were beautiful. They hadn't looked afraid the night before and they didn't look afraid now. And they looked a little less naïve.)

Inside the Convention, the bloodletting was done in a more parliamentary fashion, but was just as effective. Mayor Daley of Chicago and a nonentity by the name of John Criswell of the Democratic National Committee exercised dictatorial control over the convention proceedings. The microphones of dissident delegations were functionless when these delegations wanted the floor. Motions were peremptorily declared out of order when they were not a part of the previously laid outline for convention business. Dissident delegates were harassed by Convention guards. One delegate cried, "We're tired of being treated like sheep at this convention!" He must have also been too tired to walk out when Humphrey was nominated, because all of the dissident delegates stayed—like sheep. Complaining all the while, lamenting the death of the democratic process, they remained loyal Democrats.

Inside and outside the Convention, the liberal establishment was attacked head-on for the first time. The liberals have always been a pain to the party pros. Kennedy was a fluke which the Democrats won't repeat for a long time to come. He brought the liberals to power within the Democratic Party and with his death and Lyndon's entering the White House, liberal influence and power declined rapidly. (But let us not forget that Vietnam was a liberal's war.) With the death of the second Kennedy, the liberal wing of the Party was without a leader and without that leader, it showed itself to be ineffectual, inept, and eloquent.

Outside the Convention, the police attacked the right of dissent, the right of a free press and liberals with a zeal reminiscent of Germany, mid-thirties. And they got away with it, despite Walter Cronkite's fulminations on CBS and David Brinkley's wry witticisms on NBC. They beat whomever they wanted, including Democrats sitting in the bar of the Conrad Hilton. They even dragged people into the lobby of the hotel so they could be more comfortable while they whupped heads. They were an independent force controlled by the dictates of their consciences and the dictates of those consciences were reinforced by the silence of the Federal government.

Seventy per cent of Americans liked what they saw the police do in the parks and streets of Chicago. It was only natural that they would. Policemen lived in houses like they did, went to the churches they did, went on the same vacations they did and when policemen took off their uniforms and put on street clothes, they looked like them. It was from these people that George Wallace received an overwhelming emotional response.

### THE CANDIDATE—III

The band blared "Dixie"
and "Yankee Doodle Dandy,"
and a knot of the faithful
closed around three
silent
black demonstrators,
yelling,
"Kill'em! Kill'em! Kill'em!"
The true believers stood on their chairs,
waved rebel flags,
shook their fists in the air.
Cheers
cas-
cad-
ed
down.
Folding seats rattled
like great claps of thunder.
Violence
flick-

er-
ed
inside the hall and flared outside,
but the candidate
merely grinned
and
strutted
and threw salute
after
choppy salute at the crowd.

(*Newsweek*—November 4, 1968)

George Wallace and Richard Nixon were the only Presidential candidates to really take their campaigns to the people. While McCarthy and Kennedy had made their appeal on the basis of a humanitarian tomorrow, Hubert Humphrey thought that tomorrow would mean a return to those wonderful days of yesteryear. Wallace and Nixon came from a middle-class today, which had its defects, but a little patching here and a little patching there would get it in tip-top shape. The only difference between the two was that Wallace was too much like the people. Nixon was from them and of them, and represented confirmation of a comfortable middle class lined with bowling alleys, shopping centers and Mantovani strings which all Americans wanted. One could look at Spiro Agnew and hear Muzak. If nothing else could testify to the greatness of America, this son of a Greek immigrant could, for he was first-generation American and had risen to the governor's chair and now stood one heartbeat away from the Presidency. Who could say that hard work, clean living, and following the rules didn't pay off? (Niggers!)

Nixon represented what any American could be, any American who lived outside the big cities. Wallace represented what they were. He knew the farmer not as a statistic, but as dirt embedded in heavily-lined hands. He knew the working man not as a line on a Department of Labor graph, but as callouses and bills. Above all, George Wallace knew the bewilderment of white America at what had been happening in the country. He knew that the people didn't have a voice. Not only were they voiceless, they were without a spokesman. Blacks had Carmichael, Rap Brown, Eldridge Cleaver, Wilkins, Young and the memory of M. L. King. The New Left had Tom Hayden, Dave Dellinger, Mark Rudd, SDS and countless underground newspapers. The liberals had McCarthy, the Kennedys. These were the ones who had pushed the events of the past eight years. These were the ones who were trying to make inroads into power, trying to have not only an influence on the direction of the country, but actually wanting to control the country. The truly alienated American was not the intellectual with his existential dilemmas, not blacks, and not the young. These groups were alienated from the centers of power, but they were at least articulate and becoming organized. The vast majority of Americans were, however, silent and unknown. It was to them that George Wallace came and his message was simple and direct: "You are just one man or woman. You are just as good as he is (newspaper writers, TV men, etc.). And, in fact, the average cab driver in this country, and the beautician, the steel worker, the rubber worker, and the textile worker, knew instinctively when he saw him that Castro was a Communist. So we may be better than they are. Anyhow, there are more of us than there are of them. And we are going to show them in November that the average American is sick and tired of all those overeducated, ivory-tower folks with the pointed heads looking down their noses at us, and the left-wing liberal press writing editorials and guidelines. So we are going to shake them up in November."

Wallace shook them up, but Nixon won. America had chosen its symbol of aspiration and not the mirror. However, there was some comfort in knowing that Wallace was available for the future if Nixon failed to bring the domestic tranquility America craved.

With the election of Richard Nixon, the year came to an end, and not a minute too soon. It had been a disastrous twelve months and even if the next twelve proved to be more shattering, most Americans knew that 1968 had taught them to turn off all the machinery of response except what was necessary to make money, get ahead and make love. (How do you "MAKE *love*?") Children starving in Biafra, niggers protesting at the Olympics, strikes, planes being hijacked to Cuba, Yippies, VietnamVietnam Vietnam. Who needed it? America had precious little faith left and that little was diminished when she who had wept tears of sorrow at the funeral bier in June wept tears of joy at the altar in October.

## THE WIDOW

The scene
was the lounge of the yacht Christina.
Curtains had been pulled on all portholes
to shut out the rest of the world.
The assembled Onassis and Kennedy families,
with one or two close friends,
were preparing to have
a wedding feast.

Then, as if on cue,
other women began returning to join the assembled men.
Jean Smith came first
and caused a stir of compliments
and astonishment because she wore
silver lamé pajamas.
Then came Pat Lawford,
also in party pajamas,
and also
glittery. Hers were topped with
a tunic dotted in silver-dollar-sized
platinum trinkets.

Then,
with everyone in readiness,
and expecting the bride to come through the door,
she stepped into their midst.

She wore a floor-length white skirt,
gold shoes,
a black blouse
and the bejewelled caftan belt that the king of Morocco
gave her while she was
First Lady of the United States.

What caused everyone in the room to gasp
were the jewels,
which were so incredible

that even Mrs. Onassis' mother
found it hard to believe they were real.

On Jacqueline Onassis' left hand was
a heart-shaped cabachon
(unfaceted)
ruby
almost too large to lift.
"You couldn't dial a telephone wearing it!"
one onlooker said.
The stone was surrounded by dozens of diamonds,
each of which could make up the engagement ring
of any wealthy American woman.

On her earlobes were identical heart-shaped rubies,
of a size and quality that might come from
a treasure cask, and
they were surrounded by diamonds.
They hung from cabachon rubies
that were also surrounded by diamonds.

Caroline ran forward.
"Mummy, Mummy, Mummy!" she cried.
"They're so pretty. You're so pretty!"
Caroline held up her hand and
kept pushing her mother's long hair from the earrings
so that they were more visible.

Laughing at Caroline's pleasure in the jewels,
Jacqueline Onassis took off her ring
and gave it to her daughter to try on her own hands
and to play with like a bauble.
Caroline kept holding the ring in her hand
and tossing it in the air
so that her cousins could watch
the blazing flashes of light
as the ring tumbled.

(*Chicago Sun-Times*—October 24, 1968)

America stood exposed in 1968 for all to see and say what they were seeing. There was increasingly little middle ground to stand on. People began choosing sides and it was only a matter of time before the battle would be joined. Whether that battle would begin in one year or fifty was irrelevant. It was clear that the young were marching beneath a different flag and America was not large enough to fly two flags from the same staff.

The young were angry, but the difficulty came when they tried to articulate and create concrete programs for what they loved. Some of them went off to farms in Vermont and Oregon to set up communes. It was a solution to their problems, but revolutions only come when the means are available for everyone to solve their problems. Revolutionaries from the middle class have to be exceedingly careful, for they can too easily solve their particular problems and having done so, be content. The young needed to find the way to involve those who came from the other circles of Hell, to find the oppression which everyone had in common.

One generation cannot make a revolution. Revolution is a process of stripping away, leveling, of being worked upon and working upon. There is still a lot of poison in the soul of American man which has to be drained out before that camp can be set up from which the final guerrillas will go forth, to fight and to win. All that one generation can hope to do is proceed to the next base camp and stock it well for those who will come later.

(She had read something of mine and sent me a postcard: "Julius. I love you." And I sent her a postcard in return: "I love you, too." A few weeks later a letter came.

*what began as a quiet autumn day, turned out to be a step forward in the revolution. those few of us white militants that had about given up hope breathed deeply today and cried "viva la revolucion!" it was a great step to see hundreds united against Wallace and the pigs marching at the foot of the mountains. my thoughts turned to chicago, to newark, to our own five points, and finally to mexico where so many of our brothers and sisters are being slaughtered. there was little organization, no leadership and, an uncanny amount of fear. but we saw for the first time that there are people and those of us whose job it is to organize them will never feel so overwhelmed again. we KNOW now. Another step forward was made!*

*yours in the revolution,*

I could not share her undiluted enthusiasm, for she and I were at different places in the revolutionary process. She was young and white. I was in the shadow of thirty and ever more black. She was alive with the first glorious surges of that ecstasy which comes when one identifies with *la revolución.* I didn't know how old she was, but I didn't think she was more than twenty-one or twenty-two. When I was twenty-one, revolution was a word applied most often to what occurred in Russia in 1917. The sit-ins were just beginning and none of us could see too far beyond whatever day we awoke to. She was nine years old then and grew up watching the sit-ins, freedom rides and rebellions on television, listening to her parents and friends talk about what was happening. She stood outside the camp, watching those of us on the inside putting up tents, chopping firewood, sitting up late around the campfires. As she got older, she came closer and closer to the camp and one day, she came inside the perimeter. We hardly noticed her or those who came with her. Some of us were tired. Some of us were confused. Many of us lay in pain, having been hurt once too often. But she joined us and what for us was only another demonstration was for her that first step of joining with others. I could understand how she felt, but her feelings could not be mine. I was even a little distrustful of her feelings, because she didn't know what was to come and I couldn't help but wonder if she would last, if she would run for other shelter on those nights when the winds and the rains blew the tents over and sent them down the mountain slope. Would she help us find and untangle them and put them back up or would she hide her face when the rain, like buckshot, stung her flesh? Would she run back to the warm houses in the center of town when the rain flattened her clothes against her body, when the chill of the cold wind made her shiver beneath her one, thin blanket? I said none of this to her, because she wouldn't have understood. I wanted her to have her chance to walk at her own pace and breathe in her own rhythm. There would always be time to curse her, if that became necessary.

*eternity*

"*His heart was growing full*

*of broken wings and artificial flowers."*

*lorca*

*julius . . .*

*there are two realities, an intellectual reality and a living reality. when one leaves the living reality one gives up much of one's emotions, one's feelings of hatred, fear and maybe even hope? but the most painful part of leaving is knowing that you may never at any cost return. you may never be a peasant because you can see. not only see, but rather see too far. your sight becomes infinite and this is the tragedy.*

*when one is living in the ghetto, when one has committed oneself and death to the black revolution, when one is constantly harassed by the pigs, when the greatest reality is prison, when one can't find the money for the rent, one is a living reality. you push yourself so hard so constantly that you don't think of the intellectual lessons. it is so easy when one is a living reality, when the war continues in the ghetto 24 hours never ending.*

*i watch an image that used to be a man. i watch an image that used to be a friend. i watch an image that was love and say "you—you are the one being destroyed, manipulated, robbed of freedom and individuality. you are no longer a person." and the voice says "yes. i know, but i can't even run any more." resignation to giving your life for a "cause" is noble, but a reality that is futile.*

*i am living in the intellectual reality. i have never lived any other way. i have been cursed with intellectual reasoning. occasionally i was able to indulge in romantic adventures with che and tania and dream of giving my life for the revolution. i allowed someone to mold me into the role of a woman revolutionary of strength. and now, that person who did the molding, that person who lived with che and tania and myself, is a black panther. and julius, that is all he is. not a man, not a throbbing feeling beautiful human being, but a hate-filled blind panther. yes, he still loves me, still believes in me, even tho we can no longer work together, tho we can't even acknowledge our love in public, because of his "image." i live on the edge of the ghetto. i am not in a war. i am not being hassled by the pigs. i am not in the living reality, but he is. and he is being destroyed. WHAT DO I DO? julius, i do not believe in the reality of the "black revolution." i believe in him. i would give my life for him, but i would so much rather live my life for him. i asked once if it would be better if i left, if it would be easier on him, for i know i have the capacity to destroy. he answered "the only thing that could ever really hurt me was if you left." my 'friends' say, save yourself. get out. you're being destroyed.*

*to leave him now would be destruction for all that lives inside of me. i could never raise my head again. maybe i just need one person to say, i'm with you. you're doing the right thing. stick it out. is there hope?*

> *"the day does not wish to come
> so that you cannot come
> and i cannot go."*

*thank you.*

I wrote and said "I'm with you" because it is one's revolutionary duty to love and support those who trample through the underbrush with you. It is only a *revolutionary* duty, though, because America says that it is not a human duty and revolutionaries only come into being to keep alive the wind-twisted flames of humanness. Revolution would be unnecessary if America were human.

I could share her pain as I could not her enthusiasm as she described what being involved in *la revolución* was doing to him whom she loved. It is so hard not to hate and it is unreasonable to ask one to love those who are trying to kill you, isn't it? So one hates, but unless that hate is continually transformed into energy and that energy into action, the hate has nowhere to go and it eventually fills every organ of the body with its lethal radiation. If you're black, it is all too easy to hate white people. Indeed, it is expected of you by many. To hate white people means, *ipso facto*, that you love black people. He who hates whites, however, may only be hating the whiteness in himself, thereby not loving black people, but loving black hatred of whiteness. White people deserve to be hated. Of that there is no doubt, but hating whites is not the substance of the struggle. Neither is loving whites the substance of the struggle. Yet, if you love a white person, many blacks want to deny you a job in the revolution. But if you hate all white people, that does not mean you are revolutionary.

I know her pain and I know the pain of the black man whom she loves and who loves her. Many say that it is a contradiction to love a white person and be a black revolutionary. That is what they say. If he loves her and if it is a contradiction, I hope he is able to live with the pain of the contradiction. If he loves her, then leaves her because she is white, that hatred masquerading under the banner of revolution will have won. One hates injustice, loves humanity, and kills only because the killing is forced upon him.

I often visit the graveyard in the woods back of

the base camp to remember those whose intense
desire to love was so thwarted that their love hard-
ened and turned to hate. They were buried there,
on the edge of the camp, and I took it upon myself
to see that their graves were kept clean, for they
had so taken the pain of others into themselves, so
become a part of that "living reality" that they were
only more angered as they learned that revolution
wasn't instant, that they could not, by the sheer
strength of their wills, bring it into being. That is
the intellectual reality with which the revolutionary
must live. I sit here typing, while the majority of
my people are bent low with pain and some days I
have to tell myself that their pain would not be
eased one bit if I got up from the typewriter and
went outside and started shooting white people.
Some days I have to have the faith that sitting here
at this typewriter can be a revolutionary act with
an effectiveness equal to that of a gun. At the same
time, though, I must know that this act in which I
am engaged is no substitute for the power that only
grows from the barrel of a gun.

It is difficult and I sit among the graves and weep
for those who saw the Promised Land and did not
know that even the birds cannot fly there. Even
they must leap from limb to limb through the forests, jungles and swamps. Even they must walk over
the desert sands, through the air which holds the heat
like a lion holds the flesh of a running gazelle in its
claws.

There was little she could do. She knew one reality
and he another. His pain could not be hers and I
could only hope that he, having seen the Promised
Land, would come back to camp and help us sew

patches on our clothes and let somebody give him a massage. We needed his life, not his death, and we were only a few more than those whom we had buried.

*february 5, 1969*
*late enuf so that even*
*the city is quiet*

*dear julius*

*the candle flickering from the draft made by the open window behind my bed—cat beside me, dog on the floor and finally after weeks i feel as if i can write you honestly.*

*for the last few months i have nourished myself on the lingering illusive hope that some sunlit day he and i could escape the revolution by coming to new york, that he could escape his blackness and me my whiteness and become one with the city, thinking in some mystical way that we would not see the ghettos, hear the news or let the ugliness touch us. i realize now that i was not looking for a place to live but rather a place to hide. i watched an hour-and-a-half show on educational TV on the N.Y.C. schools and what happened/happening. i cried because my motives were so selfish and so blatantly sad. i haven't been able to speak with anyone, not even him, because i was so ashamed.*

*it seems that i must accept the reality of being the white mistress to a black revolutionary and whatever it inevitably brings. it looks as if i'll have a teacher's aide job for fall in one of the ghetto schools. there must be some hope. but being wedged between two alien worlds i do not see it.*

*we are together. each attempt at separation does nothing*

*but serve to strengthen the bond. i feel now almost as if he needs me as much or more than i him and i love him more for needing me. the time we share becomes everything. when we hold each other i keep thinking, "nothing can hurt us." julius, sometimes i'm so afraid.*

Does a day go by when I do not think, "Lord, let this cup pass from me?" Does a day go by when I do not look at those who pass me on the street and envy them their problems and their lives? I did not choose to immerse my being in the revolutionary process. I was chosen and I was told that the only reward was knowing that I was a part of the revolutionary process. I, too, am afraid, I wrote her. Afraid that one time when I am tested, I will fail. Afraid that one time when I need strength, I will not have the will to bring it into being. Sometimes it hurts so much and I am just one person and one person can't stop the world from crying. God, how I hate them! I want to live, too! I don't want to fight a revolution. I want to be happy and enjoy my children and sit in the park with Joan and write lyric poetry. God, if only they would stop hurting people, we wouldn't have to relinquish our claims to our lives. But the sun shines on the running sores of humanity and all else is irrelevant.

*march 9, 1969*
*sunny snow melting*
*afternoon*

*i feel a long julius letter coming on.*

*so much of what has happened in the last week i want to share with you. so much of the change i feel coming from inside of me.*

*ugliness was me shouting, my face contorted with hatred —pig!—fascist pig! couldn't seem to say anything else— just pig. the masses of hate-filled bodies around me, waving clenched fists, pushing eyes bright with mob fever, never daring to once steal a look at themselves. and the police glaring at us. did i once catch a glimmer in an old cop's eyes of wondering why, why a girl with soft eyes and a quiet smile could call him a bastard and spit at him and he was wondering, julius, wondering what made me hate him.*

*black and white together but irrevocably apart. each with our own hatred, reasons and realities. the black chicks literally flipping out, screaming, throwing themselves in hysterical fits, hating everything. the black men asking for a lull in the chair-throwing and violence so they could get "our black women to the back of the auditorium." i was standing beside that nameless face when he said that. i, a woman, too.*

*hayakawa, that puppet of sickness attempted to speak at the university and he became the victim of all the hostility that had dwelled within us for a lifetime. yes, i guess that it has been that long.*

*as you can probably feel by now, i am ashamed and appalled by my own ugliness and lack of intelligence. i am retreating inside myself and am returning to the world of thoughts and silent written words and self.*

*this is a synopsis of what the hayakawa fiasco taught me:*

*a) if individual movement people do not stop to think and stop hating, it will be suicidal.*

*b) if the blacks don't begin to treat white militants as intelligent equals, we shall both be destroyed.*

*c) hate is the most destructive single factor of the Revolution.*

*d) we need time and it doesn't look as if we have it.
things must slow down.*

*e) i am afraid because i understand and wish that i
didn't.*

> *the mountains send
> their love to you
> on a strain of evening
> wind.*

When I finished her letter, I knew that she would
be with us as we started the ascent toward the
plateau where we build our next camp. I was sorry
she didn't understand why a black man could not
care that she, too, was a woman, but one day she
would. We are victims, all of us now making our
way through the wilderness. We were victims before we were born and sometimes our hatred of
what was done to us threatens to destroy all that
we want to be, all that we can be. If we hate the
past more than we love the future, we will succeed
in bringing that past into the future and those who
come afterward will find our bones on the desert
sand.

I, too, am afraid, I wrote her, afraid that not
only will I not make it to the Promised Land, but
that I will forget the vision I saw from the moun-
taintop. And if we forget the vision, we have lost,
no matter how many thousands walk with us. But
how hard it is, my God how hard it is, to keep the
vision when everyone's pain has become your own.
O God God God why can't I hate them?

I can, but I mustn't.

We are not what we know we can be, but we must

not let despair immobilize us. More than anything, perhaps, the revolutionary needs faith, the faith of the Old Testament prophets, the faith of Meister Eckhart and the desert mystics, because it is only faith which will sustain us when the first excitement dies. Faith is a necessary prerequisite for commitment. It is not a blind faith, however, but a faith rooted in the knowledge that the revolution proceeds, not in an unbroken ascent, but by fits and starts. It is a faith which allows us to remove ourselves enough from events to look at them and see that what feels bad may, in essence, be good and what exhilarates us may be detrimental to the journey on which we have started. Faith will not keep us from making mistakes. It will sustain us, however, when the mistakes are inevitably made.

There is no human endeavor more difficult than the search for the New Land. Well, we shall try. We may not succeed, but we must do what we can.

Our humanity demands it of us.